PRAISE FOR *DEFYING ISIS*

Johnnie Moore has courageously focused on one of the most alarming and heartrending crises of our time. He bears witness to the war against Christianity which is being waged with horrific brutality by an evil opponent. Everyone should read this and demand their government stand up against barbarism.

—NEWT GINGRICH
FORMER SPEAKER OF THE U.S. HOUSE OF REPRESENTATIVES

This is an important book written by a competent voice at a critical time. Johnnie Moore has become one of the world's leading spokespersons for Christians in the Middle East. When most of the world didn't know about our plight—much less care—he raised his voice. Johnnie has shown in action that we are family with the suffering church. He has come with us in our suffering and pain. Even more than that, he came to our rescue. I hope millions read this book, and care enough to act.

—THE REVEREND CANON DR. ANDREW WHITE
CHAPLAIN, ST. GEORGE'S ANGLICAN CHURCH
BAGHDAD, IRAQ
WWW.FRRME.ORG

In the summer of 2014, ISIS terrorists stormed into Iraq's ancient Christian center and unleashed a genocidal jihad that exiled or killed every Christian man, woman, and child and laid waste to some of Christianity's earliest churches. Half a world away, Johnnie Moore got on a plane and rushed to the region to help. In this book, he relates the stories of the survivors he met—firsthand accounts that give vivid testimony to a powerful Christian love that prevails against satanic violence straight off a Hieronymus Bosch canvass of hell. This primer also draws links between Christian martyrs of today's Middle East and those of first century Rome, and ends with a warning to a complacent West. Every Christian in America should read it, and then help the persecuted.

—Nina Shea
Director of Hudson Institute's Center for Religious Freedom

Johnnie Moore has been consistently sounding the alarm and seeking to awaken the church in the West to the existential threat that ISIS poses to Christians in the Middle East and beyond. His timely book underscores the urgency of confronting this evil.

—Rep. Frank Wolf
Distinguished Senior Fellow
21st Century Wilberforce Initiative

I thank God for Johnnie Moore and for this important book. If Christians do not wake up to this demonic evil and take action against it, God will hold us accountable. As Dietrich Bonhoeffer said, "Silence in the face of evil is itself evil. Not to speak is to speak. Not to act is to act."

—Eric Metaxas
New York Times Bestselling Author of *Miracles* and *Bonhoeffer*

This is possibly the most important book of the year. It is not just timely and relevant—the subject makes that so—it is heartbreaking and spirit-inspiring. Written with journalistic passion, historical nuance, and Christian conviction, Moore's book doesn't need to elevate these modern martyrs to sainthood, he merely shines a light on the reality of their plight. In doing so, you realize they are the most tangible, gripping examples of the Gospel of Christ's love in our day.

—David Drury
Chief of Staff
The Wesleyan Church

DEFYING ISIS

Preserving Christianity in the Place of Its Birth and in Your Own Backyard

JOHNNIE MOORE

W Publishing Group

An Imprint of Thomas Nelson

Published in Nashville, Tennessee, by W Publishing Group, an imprint of Thomas Nelson.

Published in association with Yates & Yates, www.yates2.com.

Thomas Nelson titles may be purchased in bulk for educational, business, fund-raising, or sales promotional use. For information, please e-mail SpecialMarkets@ ThomasNelson.com.

Unless otherwise indicated, Scripture quotations are taken from the Holy Bible, New International Version®, NIV®. Copyright © 1973, 1978, 1984, 2011 by Biblica, Inc.™ Used by permission of Zondervan. All rights reserved worldwide. www.zondervan.com. The "NIV" and "New International Version" are trademarks registered in the United States Patent and Trademark Office by Biblica, Inc.™

Scripture quotations marked CEV are taken from the Contemporary English Version. Copyright © 1991, 1992, 1995 by American Bible Society. Used by permission.

Scripture quotations marked KJV are taken from The King James Version of the Bible.

Scripture quotations marked NASB are taken from the New American Standard Bible®, copyright © 1960, 1962, 1963, 1968, 1971, 1972, 1973, 1975, 1995 by The Lockman Foundation. Used by permission. (www.Lockman.org)

Library of Congress Control Number: 2015932950
ISBN 978-0-7180-3959-2

Printed in the United States of America
15 16 17 18 19 20 RRD 6 5 4 3 2 1

"The God of peace will soon crush Satan under your feet."

—ROMANS 16:20

CONTENTS

CONTENTS

PREFACE

J ust as this book was going to press, the publisher graciously allowed me to add this preface. The unrelenting stream of ISIS news compelled me to say more. The Middle East today is bursting with jihadists. They are not confined to one country, one locality, or even one organization. They can be found anywhere.

Even in the weary newsrooms that have reported one beheading after another, a new low was reached on Sunday, February 15, 2015, when ISIS warriors released a well-produced video, complete with Hollywood-style camera angles. On the shores of the Mediterranean, apparently near Tripoli, Libya, twenty-one Egyptian Coptic Christians were beheaded for their faith alone. It claimed to be prepared as "a message signed with blood to the nation of the cross." It wasn't just a message for the Middle East, it was a message sent to all Christians everywhere.

The faces of the men looked like anyone you'd see at your local coffee shop. They were young, rugged, some even handsome, with shocks of black wavy hair and olive skin tanned deeper by the sun. They were brothers, husbands, fathers from tight-knit families. They were sons. They had taken jobs in Libya to provide for their families back in Egypt.

They should still be alive, but they aren't. Their blood has polluted the Mediterranean and their twenty-one severed heads have been thrown to the wayside.

Then there was Kayla, a prep school graduate who logged hours of volunteer work in her hometown of Prescott, Arizona. Kayla had a quick laugh, a huge heart, and a focus on the world. She graduated college with a political science degree in 2009. As classmates polished their resumes, she packed her bags. Graduates her age looked for a way to start their career. Kayla started hers spending most of the next two years in India and Israel, volunteering in hope of relieving the suffering of other people. When she did return home, she went to work at an AIDS clinic and an area women's shelter.

After a year at home, Kayla spent another year in France to learn the language. Then, Kayla saw an opportunity to go to Turkey to ease the suffering of refugees from the surrounding war-ravaged region. Like any twenty-something, Kayla skyped with her boyfriend. She wrote letters to family and friends. She laughed and posed for pictures. She seized every opportunity to help. That's what led Kayla to Syria on August 3, 2013, to see how she could assist Doctors Without Borders. The next day, extremists kidnapped her.

For the next eighteen months, Kayla's family received occasional communication that she was alive. Then, on February 10, 2015, Kayla's grieving family released a statement confirming their daughter had been executed. In the last letter they received, Kayla wrote, "I remember Mom always telling me that all in all, in the end, the only one you really have is God. I have come to a place in experience where, in every sense of the word, I have surrendered myself to our Creator because literally there was no one else."

It is with Kayla's concluding words that I start this book:

"I have a lot of fight left inside of me. I am not breaking down and I will not give in no matter how long it takes. . . . Do not fear for me, continue to pray, as will I, and by God's will, we will be together soon."

INTRODUCTION

The dictionary defines *martyr* as "a person who is killed because of their religious or other beliefs." In the sixteenth century, a Christian "book of martyrs" was famously compiled by John Foxe to insure that subsequent generations of Christians would never forget the tragic stories of those who had given life and limb for the cause of Christ. Foxe begins his classic with these words:

"(The) Church has endured and held its testimony of Christ through every attack brought against it. Its passage through the storms caused by violent anger and hate has been glorious to see, and much of its history is written in this book so that the wonderful works of God might be to Christ's glory and that the knowledge of the experiences of the Church's martyrs might have a beneficial effect upon its readers and strengthen their Christian faith."[1]

Foxe's book has been passed down through generations of Christians. Millions have read and told its stories, and told them as legends from a bygone era. We have celebrated their faith and heroism, and thanked God that we didn't live in an era where our faith might cause us to be thrown to lions, crucified, beheaded, sold as slaves, impaled on stakes, or buried alive.

Yet, as a shame to our modern world, this barbarism persists; history is replaying itself in places like Iraq and in Syria, and we're witnessing a new *Foxe's Book of Martyrs* being written every single day at the hands of terrorists who intend on giving both Christians, and everyone else, one option: *convert or die.*

This is not an imagined or exaggerated crisis, but a very real one.

It's apparent in the news headlines. It's present in our nightmares, in the unexpected questions of our children, and in the franticness with which the most powerful leaders in the world are scrambling to address the guerilla nature of a jihadist war that waxes on at the hands of a stateless enemy—whose psychopathic supporters exist in New York, Paris, and Toronto, as they do in Al-Raqqa and Mosul.

The threat facing us is the threat of a thousand kinds of Nazis spread throughout the entire globe without a single vein of conscience restraining their evil. The terror of it all is that these arbiters of hate aren't confined to a Third Reich. They are dispersed in every corner of the world, quietly "sleeping" in their cells, awaiting the order or opportunity to shed innocent blood to strike terror in us all.

Every drop of innocent blood prompts their celebration to the world's horror, and every ounce of fear fuels their unbridled evil.

Perhaps at the hands of the strong and good in our world these terrorists will eventually realize—as previous generations of terrorists have—that "love is . . . more powerful than death."[2]

But, between now and then, their hate will rage wildly across the globe, particularly targeting Christians.

They will not win their fight to eradicate the world of Christianity, nor will they win their war with the West, but they might very well win their fight to eradicate the Middle East of it. Through it all have arisen stories of men, women, and children who have given everything for their faith, even their lives, and stories of those who when facing inevitable death lifted their eyes to their God in hope that good will eventually triumph over this evil. The terror they endured jarring the world from its lethargy.

Here I will tell some of their stories so that the world will have the opportunity to remember those who stared down the hell of ISIS with the love of Jesus. I'll also attempt to guide us as to what we can do to combat this threat across the world and in our own backyard.

I've written these words because I've learned to love this browbeaten part of the world with the deepest part of me, and I've found endless hope in its beautiful people—Muslim, Christian, Yazidi, Mandean, Turkmen, and Kakai—whose lives have been swept up in conflicts they didn't choose and wars they couldn't stop.

I once didn't know their stories, and was embarrassingly uneducated on all that Christians, in particular, have contributed to a region of the world that I thought was entirely Islamic. Thankfully, I was educated by Muslim friends in the Middle East on all that their Christian neighbors have done in the region for two thousand years. All of that contribution now threatened by people who manipulate religion as a means to behead journalists, sell children as sex slaves, burn prisoners of war alive, throw people off buildings, and leave no debauchery to imagination in their attempt to forcibly convert—or kill—anyone that stands in their way.

The stories of those who have defied them with courage and faith will inspire us, and they will shame us for doing so little, so late, in this time of such great need.

They will also warn us to awaken to this threat slithering its way through the dark corners of our broken world, for *the ambition of these maniacs is to do here what they've done there.*

They aim to make the West the killing fields that they have made the Middle East, and to ensure that no one who disbelieves in their perverted ideology will have the opportunity to preach their own.

Their faith is not an Islamic one, but a satanic one.

The threat of ISIS is a threat to the livelihood of every sensible person on the planet, and in its crosshairs is the faith of the world's two billion Christians and nearly all of its Muslims, Jews, Hindus, and Buddhists.

If they have their way, you won't live another day.

There's nothing in the world truer than that.

That's why you should read this book.

PART ONE

———— ◆ ————

WHAT ISIS
IS DOING

1

BURN THEIR CHURCHES AND KILL THEIR PASTORS

It was midnight in Damascus, 2:00 p.m. in my hometown in California, when I received an e-mail with only two words in its subject line: "Awaiting death."

The sender of the message was in Syria, and while I had heard of him, I had never met him. Yet, somehow, I felt eerily close to him. He was a faithful Christian pastor who hadn't a vein of violence in his body. But what he did have was love for those he'd served for so long—a love that waged on despite the hatred encompassing his city.

There once were many pastors like him in Syria. That country's Christian communities had thrived since Paul himself preached in Damascus after his conversion on the road to that ancient city. In fact, it was in Syria that the word "Christian" was first used at all.

Within the Middle East, Syria was once as famous for its

---

two million Christians as it was for anything else. They were pillars of society, living and thriving as neighbors to Muslims whom they served without prejudice. Their mysterious hillside monasteries had maintained the same intrigue they had when they were first constructed, many more than a thousand years ago.

Syria was so Christian, in fact, that a certain group of Syrian Christians had preserved Aramaic—the very dialect that Jesus had spoken. They spoke it in their communities and people traveled from the world over to their villages just for the opportunity to hear the Lord's Prayer prayed exactly as it had been heard from Jesus' lips to his apostles' ears, two thousand years ago.

Until our very modern times, Syria, along with Iraq and Egypt, were the seats of thriving Christian communities that had been a light to the world before Western Christianity was a glimmer in anyone's eye. As I wrote in an op-ed in February of 2014:

> Christianity began in the East, not the West . . . the apostle Paul—who was on the road to Damascus when he encountered Christ—would have told the story of his conversion while heading to "Syria." . . . and to this day there are as many Christian holy sites in that nation as anywhere else in the world.[1]

The pastor that e-mailed me that evening now lived in a very different Syria. He lived in a Syria ripped to shreds by war;

a Syria whose ancient Christian populations lay decimated in its wreckage and blood.

He wrote me that night from a city—once famous for its thousands of Christians—now made famous for the brutality of its conflict. He wrote me from a city whose streets were lined with dead bodies, whose buildings had been reduced to rubble, and whose future was as bleak as any place on the planet.

He was one of the last surviving Christians, and to this day I have no idea whether he survived.

He simply couldn't let himself leave when everyone else had fled, or died, in the war. This city was his home. There were still people there to care for, and he was God's shepherd to those people. And as we've all been taught from lessons that go all the way back to biblical times, shepherds struggle with the thought of leaving a single sheep behind.

If one sheep lies wounded, a shepherd is conditioned to fight with all his might for that one—and this shepherd stood in a blood bath of meticulous and intentional destruction by the very incarnation of hell itself born in the brutality of the Islamic State of Iraq and Syria (ISIS—also sometimes referred to as ISIL, the Islamic State, or, in Arabic, as DAESH).

The absolute horror in his voice screamed off the page, as I read what he had written in an e-mail using his cell phone sent during the middle of a terrifying night:

I am here in my room sitting in darkness because we now only receive one hour of electricity per day. It's around midnight. I'm waiting here with others in my building as we play hide and seek with death.

As I write, another two mortars just fell on the building in front of us, another on the building to the right, and another one on the building on the next street over.

So far, we have been spared.

But are we next?

When will it be our turn?

Should I just stay in my bed so that I'll die in peace, or should I go to the ground floor of the building so that I might be able to escape?

But how long should I stay here?

Should I try and sleep or is it better to stay awake to feel the moment when Death comes riding on one of these mortars?

Wow!

Just now, it finally hit us.

Shaking this big building I am living in.

The windows pushed out violently, and I can hear horrifying screams from everywhere, all around me. Yet, except for the flash of light, there are no lights.

I can't even see what's going on.

I can only hear it.

I think I've decided it's better to stay in my room and await death.

Another mortar just hit . . .

I'm just going to be quiet.

What happened to that pastor that night was not an accident. He didn't get caught in the cross fire unintentionally. He was a casualty of a war that was meant to take his life.

The goal of ISIS from the very beginning has been to ethnically cleanse their land, and eventually the world, of Christians. Their hatred doesn't end with Christians, they also intend on wiping out all moderate Sunni Muslims, Shiites, and every member of ancient religious minority sects like the Yazidis. Their hate knows no bounds and their mission has been relentlessly and successfully pursued.

But make no mistake, they take particular joy in killing Christians.

CHURCHES ARE NOT places where people ought to bleed to death because of bullet wounds. Mothers ought not be sold into sexual slavery, along with their nine-year-old daughters. And Christians—and their priests and pastors—ought not be threatened, robbed, harassed, kidnapped, crucified, tortured, or even beheaded because they simply cared for the poor of their community in the name of Jesus.

Yet, on any given day in Iraq over the last ten years, these horrors have played themselves out thousands of times. Just when no one believed things could get any worse, our world has watched as the barbarism of ISIS has made its fatal march across an already-battered Iraq. ISIS has brought an incarnation of hell itself into monasteries and churches, the homes of peace-loving believers, and on the streets of ancient cities where the severed heads of all those who've stood in their way are routinely on display.

ISIS has arrived in our modern time with a premodern cruelty that our world has mostly forgotten. At its very core is an unrelenting hatred for Christianity, and other religious minorities, that seeks their total extinction whether they live in Iraq, Syria, or in the United States. They also hate those who actually follow the Islam that ISIS professes guides them, and have killed more Muslims than anyone else.

They will stop at nothing and would willingly sacrifice their own lives to take the lives of all who do not submit to their ideology. If you live in any metropolitan city in the world, you can rest assured that they aren't far away. They are there, quietly biding their time, awaiting their opportunity to shed innocent blood.

They represent an affront to every sensible thing in our

modern world, and they will leave our world a place of unrestrained horror if they have their way.

Just ask those who were worshipping at the Our Lady of Salvation church in Baghdad on October 31. On this particular morning, the number of dead totaled fifty-eight, with blood so far-flung that it had stained the ceiling. Islamic radicals who were dressed as security guards had taken the entire church hostage. When they locked the doors, the bloodletting began.

One elderly woman watched as her seventy-year-old husband gasped for his last breath. Another woman rocked between wailing and silence as she stood in the church's crypt next to her daughter who was both newly married and newly pregnant, and now newly dead.

Two of those who had been killed were priests.

Jane Arraf, the courageous reporter who rushed into the havoc told Public Radio International, "There are so many to be buried, the graveyard manager tells the families that they only have five minutes each."[2]

One of those she met in the chaos put it simply: "There is no future for Christians in Iraq."[3]

He may have been right.

The men, women, and children there were targeted on that day for one single reason: their Christian faith. And who were those who claimed responsibility?

The Islamic State of Iraq under its newly appointed leader, Abu Bakr al-Baghdadi . . . that's who.

But this was not in 2014 or 2015 as ISIS marched from village to city massacring the innocent along the way. The October 31–church massacre in Baghdad was in 2010, a full four years before ISIS captured one contiguous piece of Iraqi and Syrian land the size of the United Kingdom.[4] This was years before the ISIS guerilla war had recruited as many as two hundred thousand serial killers[5] with the intent of hunting Christians, Yazidis, and others, and slaughtering them with less care than butchers give to sheep. This was a half-decade before ISIS was collecting between 1.6 and 3.5 million dollars a day selling oil on the black market, allowing them to pay their mercenary fighters salaries that doubled the average income for most people in the region.[6]

Yet, this much-publicized attack in 2010 wasn't even the beginning. As Nina Shea of the Hudson Institute notes, between 2003 and the arrival of ISIS, the Iraqi Christians were subjected to a myriad of "deliberate church bombings and assaults, as well as assassinations, an epidemic of kidnappings, and other attacks against clergy and laity alike. In recent years, particularly since 2004, a million of Iraq's Christians have been driven out of the country by such atrocities. This can be rightly called targeted religious cleansing, and it is a crime against humanity."[7]

In Baghdad alone, since 2003, forty of the city's sixty-five churches have been bombed. In all, more than one hundred churches across Iraq, many of them ancient churches where Christians have worshipped continually for centuries, have been attacked, bombed, or destroyed entirely. Presently, every church in the country that is still operating has constructed a wall around the building. The walls are "blast walls" so that the effect of car bombs can be diminished because it's no longer a matter of "if" but a matter of "when" they'll be attacked.

For many years there were warning signs everywhere that these radicals had one intended goal: wiping out Christianity entirely from the region of its birth. The world stood quietly by while Iraq's population of 1.5 million Christians was picked off one by one. Now, at best, only 10 percent remain, and they remain living lives of quiet desperation.

The ISIS plan is becoming reality as the dreams of two-thousand-year-old Christian communities lie in rubble between the Tigris and Euphrates. The place where God first made man is the place where evil men are attempting to use the name of God to destroy mankind.

Yet, after a decade of warnings and an unrestrained escalation of threats, the remaining Christians still hold their faith dear, refusing to convert, and therefore choosing to die.

The few that have survived waste away in refugee camps—having traded their secure livelihoods for makeshift tents. They have been forced to exchange their homes for a ramshackle existence. Their faith cost them everything, and yet, they adorn their decrepit dwellings with a cross—raised high into the sky and lined with lights to make sure the terrorists know they still hold on to it all.

While their reality seems so entirely separate from our own, and while it might seem unimaginable, the fact is that the same ideology that has nearly destroyed them is incubating in our country and in every country in the world.

Their reality could be our reality more quickly than any of us realize.

The threat of ISIS isn't just a threat to our Christian brothers and sisters in Iraq and Syria. It is a threat to every one of us on planet earth. It's already rearing its fierce head, and if they cannot find a way to enslave us, they will find a way to make us live in perpetual fear. It's only a matter of time. If something significant doesn't change very quickly, the churches and Christian communities in the West will become ground zero in their attempt to rid the world of those who will not embrace their deformed ideology.

It only takes one ISIS sympathizer to turn your church, school, business, or community into the frontlines of their global jihad.

THE ISIS PLAN to rid the world of Christians isn't clandestine. It's not a carefully guarded secret confined to quiet meetings behind closed doors. It's not even a dream to be realized only when the Islamic State has consumed the entire world. On the contrary, ISIS is so dedicated to perpetrating a Christian holocaust that they talk about it boldly and often.

In fact, in October 2014, the cover photo of the magazine published by ISIS was a picture of St. Peter's Square in the Vatican. With utter and complete audacity, ISIS had superimposed their chilling black jihadist flag on the ancient Egyptian obelisk that adorns the center of St. Peter's Square. Their cover article promised to "break the crosses" and "trade and sell the women" of the Christians. In every public appearance or written statement by Abu Bakr al-Baghdadi—the infamous leader of ISIS—he mentions specifically that they intend to march all the way to Rome. It is noteworthy that he didn't select New York City, Paris, or London. The plan at the heart of the ISIS threat is to plant their radicalism into the heart of St. Peter's Square, and to raise their black flag over one of the cities that most symbolizes Christianity.[8]

They would revel in the opportunity to have the Pope endure the same fate as St. Peter himself, and then behead every priest and parishioner in a grotesque display of power and terror. They would love to put the severed heads of those working in the Vatican atop Bernini's sculptures lining St. Peter's Square. They would turn St. Peter's Square into a river of "infidel" blood and its Basilica into a mosque, after raiding the Vatican's museum and archives.

They would crush her ancient statues, burn her priceless art, and turn the Sistine Chapel into a market for sex slaves, or a prison for those awaiting execution. The executions would take place prominently, publicly in St. Peter's square. The leader of ISIS would take the Papal apartment as his home with the entire world as his goal.

This isn't a far-fetched dream they aim to realize. This is a rock-solid goal they are pursuing at this very moment, and they believe entirely that they are capable of executing their plan. ISIS is unabashed at their desire to eliminate Christianity all together.

This isn't just a *part* of their plan.

It is the heart of it.

While those who are fighting ISIS are not engaged in a religious war, ISIS is very much engaged in a religious war—using religion as a means to kill the innocent in order to gain more power for themselves.

Or, as Baghdadi said himself in a seventeen-minute audio recording released by ISIS this winter, "Be assured, O Muslims, for your [Islamic] state is good and in the best condition. Its march will not stop and it will continue to expand, by Allah's permission. The march of the mujahidin [Muslim holy warriors] will continue until they reach Rome."[9]

The church that took two thousand years to build in Iraq and Syria, started by the apostles themselves, has nearly been destroyed in the blink of an eye at the hands of maniacs who won't stop until they win or they die.

At least that's what everyone I met in Iraq believes. *Every single one of them.*

FOR CENTURIES, BEING appointed archbishop of Mosul was considered among the greatest honors in the Christian church. The roots of Christianity in Mosul run all the way back to the first century when the ancient, indigenous Assyrian community converted to Christianity. Mosul is also the biblical city of Nineveh where the Prophet Jonah preached and Jonah's own tomb remained an ancient symbol of the city's heritage of faith until ISIS blew it to smithereens on July 25, 2014.

That same July, ISIS militants distributed notices all around this ancient city notifying its Christians that they must convert to Islam in just a few days or face death "by sword."

That notice—which I have a picture of, being held by one of those who received it—read in part:

> After notice to the heads of the Nasirites [Christians], and their followers, for the date to appear to clarify their situation under the shadow of the Islamic State in the province of

Nineveh, they objected and failed to appear at the appointed time designated for them earlier. It had been decided that we would put before them one of three choices:

1. Islam;
2. The Covenant of the Dhimma (and this means the taking of jizya [tax] from them);
3. If they decline that, then there is nothing left but the sword.

The Commander of the Faithful, the Caliph Ibrahim, God strengthen him, has shown benevolence by permitting them to evacuate—by themselves only—to the borders of the Islamic caliphate no later than noon Saturday. . . . After that date, there is nothing between us and them but the sword.[10]

They had three options.

They could convert, pay an excessive tax, or face the sword.

ISIS preferred to exercise the latter option, and as the Nazis did with the Star of David, the militants then began to mark the homes of Christians in the city by spray-painting the Arabic letter "N" (for Nazarene, the word for Christian) on them in red.

Thus, the countdown to death began and the Christians began to flee the city by the thousands. They left in such haste because ISIS was already beginning their massacre, unconstrained by their own rules, and determined to totally rid that ancient Christian city of anyone who would not convert. It was the middle of the searing Iraqi summer, so many of them left with only a T-shirt on their backs, expecting to return to their home very soon, once the West eliminated ISIS. They were totally oblivious to the fact that they might have to endure the frigid Iraqi winter with only the clothes on their backs. As I write these words, the refugee camps are blanketed in snow.

When I met Daoud Matti Sharaf, Metropolitan of the Syriac Orthodox Church of Mosul, he was living in Erbil where he and his flock had fled to save their lives. Sharaf is a jovial fellow, rotund with a bright-red beard and a benevolent fierceness about him. He's the type of person who is best described as "straightforward," always telling you what is on his mind. He is a strong man, but beaten down. As I looked at his slouching shoulders, once broad and straight, he reminded me of the words of the apostle Paul:

> We are hard pressed on every side, but not crushed; perplexed, but not in despair; persecuted, but not abandoned; struck down, but not destroyed. We always carry around in our body the death of Jesus, so that the life of Jesus may also be revealed in our body. For we who are alive are always being given over to death for Jesus' sake, so that his life may

also be revealed in our mortal body. So then, death is at work in us, but life is at work in you.[11]

I asked the Metropolitan how they were doing, and he answered, "We have no hope. Only God. We will not return to Mosul unless there is international protection. [People in the West] say they do not know. How can you *not* know? You either support ISIS or you have turned off all of the satellites. I am sorry to say this but my pain is big. I am an archbishop, and I have no churches. I am not afraid of anything. I have lost everything."

Had they not fled they would have been left to a horrific fate. A nun named Christine told me, "If we had stayed, they would have done to us what they have done everywhere else: bury women alive, or sell them into slavery, while taking the young boys to the madrassas. We feel like we are living a nightmare. We wake up every morning and wonder if this is true?"

Unfortunately, it is true.

Or in the words of an elderly Christian woman I met in Iraq, "Christianity in Iraq is bleeding . . . we are extremely exhausted . . . every day we hope tomorrow will be better, but our tomorrows seem to bring only more tears and more hardship . . . When will you rescue us?"

A once-in-a-thousand-year threat to Christianity is being waged wildly in the heart of the birthplace of Christianity.

And the world sleeps . . .

PATRIARCHS AND PROPHETS

He grew up in Iraq.

Since it was the land of his birth, he was always comfortable with its surroundings, its customs, and its people. Its sights, its sounds, its tastes, and its smells. Sure, the Iraqi population had gotten a lot of bad press—even back then—but he was content to remain in that country as long as he lived, because that's what people did back then.

But his God had other ideas.

God wanted him to go to another country. To make the request even more intriguing, God didn't identify the country by name. Just pick up and leave. To paraphrase God's command, "Young man, go from Iraq, from your family of origin, from the house you grew up in, and go to a place that I will show you. But know that I will bless you. I will make you famous. I will make you into a great nation" (see Genesis 12:1–2).

This is not a promise that God made four hours ago, four days ago, or four years ago, but *four thousand years ago.* We have left the current scene in Iraq and are visiting the historical. In this particular case, we are, of course, talking about the great patriarch of the Old Testament named Abraham.

Historically, not all of God's people were told to leave Iraq. Some were told just the opposite—to go there.

Another man, a different man, was living a happy, contented life in Palestine. Let's call him Joe. This man Joe grew up in Palestine, and like Abraham's early years in Iraq, he never thought he would leave the country of his birth.

But God had other plans.

"Arise, go to Nineveh (modern Mosul), the great city, and cry against it, for their wickedness has come up before Me" (see Jonah 1:2), God solemnly declared to this man.

Nineveh, however, was a scary destination to this person. Joe wanted to obey his God, but he didn't want to put his very life in jeopardy. Those Ninevites did awful things to people they viewed as their enemies. And our man feared he would be viewed as their enemy.

So Joe devised an escape plan.

He arranged to board a ship that was docked to the west of Palestine in a tiny port town called Joppa. He wanted to silently slip away, and he knew this ship would be perfect for his plan because it wasn't sailing anywhere near Nineveh. In fact, it was going the exact opposite direction.

This ship was heading to Spain, as far away from Nineveh as he could get.

Two thousand miles west of Palestine.

Near the Rock of Gibraltar (perhaps Joe thought he could hide from God behind that famous rock?).

The exact site back then was called Tarshish, but it's not real important because our friend never made it there. By now, you've probably got it figured out, right? We're referring to the Old Testament prophet, whose full name was Jonah. His trip to Tarshish was abruptly detoured when Jonah was thrown out of the ship and swallowed by the great fish.

And all of this drama because he wasn't willing to go to Iraq.

Just as so many of the Christians I know in the West who are so unwilling to turn their attention to our brothers and sisters living in the East.

We're still refusing to go to Nineveh, and I hear God saying to us as he said to Jonah, "Should I not be concerned for that great city of Nineveh?"[12]

2

SLAUGHTER THEM OR MAKE THEIR CHILDREN SOLDIERS

The city's name is Qaraqosh.

It was sometimes called "Iraq's Christian capital." So to ISIS it was a fishbowl. They could eliminate as many Christians as possible—in one fell swoop—ridding their Islamic State of these "infidels."

Along the way, they could enslave the strong ones, traffic the beautiful ones, and steal everything worth anything. Their mandate was to show no mercy, and to kill everyone who stood against them as terrifyingly as possible.

And there's no better way to instill terror than to abuse the women and children. So, they did it in fury.

Mazen knows this horror on a personal level. His family wasn't able to get out before the ISIS attack began. He is a tall, thin man of middle age with deep-set eyes and leathery skin that tells us he has spent hours working in the sun. Considered a highly respected man in the community, Mazen once held his head high, but not anymore. The agonies of the attacks have weighed down on him and his once-strong posture is now a humbled crouch in a naked room of gray slab. Mazen recounts the horror of the morning ISIS arrived:

[It was] nine in the morning when a mortar landed on our house. My son died. My nephew was hit in the head. My other son remains wounded, and our neighbor next door died. . . . We fled, all of us. . . . My other son, Milad, died on the way. I have another son who needs an operation. . . . It costs $15,000.' Where would I get that? We don't have a house or property or anything [anymore].

Mazen's son was nine years old when he died, and his nephew was four. He showed us three-by-five color photographs of the boys, clad in colorful shirts and khaki shorts, full of smiles, life, and vigor. In our interview with the family, I quickly lost track of all the deaths as other family members began to insert their own stories. They were heartbreaking narratives, describing children "blown to pieces" in the streets, mothers who died awful deaths within earshot of their families, and the little boy who was seen carrying bits of flesh in his hands, just trying to help someone, somehow, while teetering himself on the edge of sanity.

Ahmed is another one of those lives that ISIS has destroyed. Except, unlike Mazen's children, he doesn't really understand how life is supposed to be to begin with. He's only five years old. He's one of his parents' six children, and they lived in an idyllic village in Northern Iraq. Before ISIS, Ahmed was a jovial child filled with creativity and adventure. He was fun and always full of words.

"Now," Ahmed's uncle tells us, while shaking his head sadly, "he has seen too many horrors to overcome them."

When ISIS came to his village, which they targeted specifically because it was the home of Christians, they began to senselessly massacre people in cold blood. They were killing Christians in the streets. What five-year-old Ahmed observed in his quiet little town traumatized him so deeply that he has lost his ability to talk. His cheerful personality has been reduced to a stone-faced glare, lost in his own mind. His mother wants to add to the story, but her words stick in her throat. Her deep brown eyes well up with tears as she can't help but weep uncontrollably while making a brave effort to tell this emotional story.

Her son is alive, she tells me with large hand expressions in front of her taut-muscled face, but he is dead inside. The trauma has tunneled so deeply into his psyche that he might never recover. The glaze in his mother's own expression leads me to believe she is in a very similar condition.

The evil of ISIS isn't inhibited by the innocence of children.

On the contrary, they prey upon the innocence of children. Rather than shielding children from the war they have started, they welcome the opportunity to place them right in the middle of it. When they find a child, they revel in the chance to inflict a particular type of horror into the hearts of those they hate. They sincerely believe they are doing a justice by ridding the world of another generation of Christians, and so they massacre them with pure joy.

There is nothing of which ISIS is incapable. Take a moment to read this letter I received one evening from deep within ISIS territory:

A friend [of mine] just got a text message from her brother asking her to shower him and his parish in prayer. ISIS took over the town they are in today. He said ISIS is going from house-to-house to all the Christians and asking their children to denounce Jesus. He said so far not one child has. And so far all [the children] have consequently been killed, but not the parents . . . he said he is very afraid and has no idea how to even begin ministering to these families who have seen their children martyred. Yet, he says he knows God has called him for some reason to be His voice and hands at this place at this time. . . . He is asking us to pray for his courage to live out his faith in such dire circumstances, and—like the children—accept martyrdom if he is called to do so. . . . These brave parents instilled such a fervent faith in their children that they chose martyrdom. Please surround them in their loss with your prayers for hope and perseverance.

The imposing and sanguine Vicar of Baghdad, Canon Andrew White, told a similar story to his congregation one Sunday morning. His story came from a village not far from Baghdad where members of ISIS demanded four children to "convert to Islam, or die." Not a single child was willing to deny their faith in Jesus Christ and convert to ISIS and their perverted form of Islam. Not a single child. So, not a single child survived.

"So," Canon White said with the tears breaking through his composed persona, "they beheaded all of them."

Canon White then wept, unable to control his tears, he continued to preach through them:

"They were all *our* children. That is how evil these people are. So evil. They have no respect for anyone. The other day they chopped a four-year-old boy in half. He didn't do anything. What can a four-year-old boy do? He was just a boy."[2]

That little boy White was speaking of was also named Andrew.

His parents were members of the church White shepherded in Baghdad, and they loved their pastor so dearly that they named their child after him, never imagining their child would become a Christian martyr. Canon Andrew White had even baptized little Andrew never knowing that little boy would be cut in half because of all that baptism symbolized.

The ISIS atrocities against children are as numerous as they are incomprehensible. Senator Dianne Feinstein, the then Chairman of the Senate Intelligence Committee, said in September 2014:

> I have a picture of what I estimate to be a six-year-old girl in a gingham party dress, white tights, a little red band around her wrist, Mary Janes [shoes], and she's lying on the ground, and her head is gone . . . this could be an American child. It could be a European child. It could be a child anywhere. . . . They have killed thousands; they are marching on.[3]

Then there's Aida, a quiet young mother with a beautiful three-year-old daughter. Like most of those who lived in Qaraqosh, her family had been Christian for generations. Almost no one in her town can remember a time when Aida's family wasn't Christian. Their community was one of the oldest Christian communities in the world. They were wonderful people who lived in peace with all of their neighbors.

It was four in the morning when ISIS arrived to their town in their black clothes, waving their black flags, shooting their guns in the air as they shouted "God is great!"

Then, they began to shout something different.

Knowing they were in a Christian city, they began to scream "CHRISTIANS! Leave before we behead you." They laughed as they yelled, but it wasn't a laugh of jokesters. It was the sinister laugh of serial killers. The laugh of those who smile while they chop you to bits.

Aida told us:

> We were waiting for the situation to improve and hoping that safety and security would return. The situation, though, deteriorated day-by-day, and [then] after ten days we were being threatened. They were telling us to convert to Islam, or leave. We were under house arrest . . . they took our gold and money and even our extra clothing.

Then, as if stealing their gold wasn't enough, ISIS decided to steal something far more dear to them—their three-year-old daughter, Christina. They piled the three of them on a bus. They didn't know at the time, but they would soon drop them outside of town—leaving them to flee or die. But before they did, they decided to inflict one final injustice. They sent someone onto the bus to yank Christina out of her mother's arms.

"I begged them to give her back to us. I asked over and over and they refused," Aida said. She ran off the bus, chasing after her dear daughter and screaming at the top of her lungs.

Then they grabbed Aida, throwing her back on the bus, explaining that they were being merciful to not kill her on the spot.

They then drove them outside of town, dropping them off in the middle of the desert where they walked seven hours to the nearest town, wondering all along the way about the fate of their daughter. Aida said, "We don't know why they took our daughter . . . she was the only child left in Qaraqosh. . . . We don't know what happened to her. . . . As a mother I'm going through torture. I'm always thinking about her. I can't eat or sleep. . . . I keep seeing her in my dreams."

A tear just hit my keyboard as I finished typing that last sentence.

My eyes are so full of tears that I almost can't see this computer screen in front of me. I wish I could say that this story is an exception—that this story is an anomaly, or that it is "unusual" or an "isolated incident." But the fact of the matter is that ISIS has again and again intentionally targeted children in horrific ways.

The order to take Christina that day didn't come from an underling that was pursuing his own vile ends; it came from the "emir" in charge that day. Aida and her family tried everything in their power to rescue Christina. In desperation, they even tried to "buy her back" through a representative pleading that she was their only child. Yet, with hearts as stone-cold as the evil they perpetrate, the ISIS militants defiantly refused the family's pleading and sent them off to nowhere with nothing, not even their little girl.

It's a blight on the entire planet that the world doesn't wail at this barbarism, for these children are indeed "our" children, and the world ought to be rising up in rage at the atrocities of these evil men. On the contrary, we let ISIS take "our" children as spoils of war.

Imagine if they were actually *our own children?*

ISIS IS GUILTY of more than kidnapping, selling, and trading children. ISIS also summarily *executes* children. The most conservative estimates put the number of executed children in Syria alone at more than ten thousand. In the village of al-Tleiliye in Northern Syria seven children, between the ages of one and twelve, were murdered in a single attack. Their families were working on land owned by a family who practiced an ancient religion akin to Zoroastrianism called Yazidism. The ISIS hatred for Christianity is only eclipsed by their hatred of the ancient Yazidis, and they just can't bear the thought of a Yazidi prospering. Therefore, they had embarked upon the task of ridding the village of "infidels."

An eyewitness found the slain children when he arrived in

the village. He slipped into a nondescript house and was nearly knocked to the floor by the smell of decaying bodies. There were two murdered women lying there, and between them lay the dead body of a five-year-old boy. The whole farm was a horror movie. Another woman lay dead in a pickup truck alongside three other children. Then there were two men lying dead on the dirt. Yet another man's corpse was leaning against the wall of a house, having been shot in the head. In addition, there were four bodies in a car, including a little eleven-year-old girl.[4]

The children who died that day were one, three, five, seven, two were eleven, and one was twelve years old. Their names were Mohammed, Hussein, Mohammed, Ibrahim, Asmaa', Khaled, and Sahar.

Their fate has been faced by another ten thousand, all of which were innocent, none of which were even raising arms to defend their own property. Their only "crime" was their religion. ISIS' plan being to wipe out the next generation.

There are as many horrifying stories as there are children whom ISIS has encountered. In the Syrian city of Kobani, they abducted more than 150 Kurdish boys between the ages of fourteen and sixteen, beating them ruthlessly with hoses and electric cables.

They forced them to memorize misinterpreted religious sayings. If they weren't able to perfectly recite them they were beaten more. One of the boys who escaped said they asked them for addresses of family members so that they might "get them and cut them up."[5]

In the Syrian city of Raqqa, the "capital of the Islamic State," children were forcibly enrolled in ISIS-controlled "training camps" where they were taught how to decapitate people. One of those was a thirteen-year-old boy named Mohammad. His mother explained,

> After his return [from camp] his mother says she was surprised to find in his bag a blond, blue-eyed doll—along with a large knife given to her son by his ISIS supervisors. When she confronted Mohammad, he told her that the camp manager had distributed the dolls and asked that the children decapitate them using the knife, and that they were asked to cover the dolls' faces when they performed the decapitation. It was his homework: practice beheading a toy likeness of a blond, white Westerner.[6]

Brainwashed children have been forced to join the ISIS army as "Cubs of the Islamic State," and "instead of archery and merit badges . . . these boys learn how to clean, dissemble, and shoot machine guns . . . 'They make them watch a beheading, and sometimes they force them to carry the heads in order to cast the fear away from their hearts.'"[7] Child soldiers are sometimes used as human shields or are forced to become suicide bombers.[8]

In a little-publicized video from a playground in Syria, an ISIS teacher is recorded threatening to kill the children if they don't comply. He says he will cut them as they slaughter sheep.

In a much more publicized video, a "Cub of the Islamic State"—probably twelve years old—shoots two ISIS prisoners in the head at point-blank range. The child has a stoic look on his face, already drained of his natural human proclivities and manipulated into becoming a murderer. He has long dark hair and eyes that are as black as night. He strikes terror in you as you look at him there with his ISIS overlord looking approvingly on as he executes those who have chosen not to believe.

The stories go on and on.

The United Nations Human Rights Commission "has received numerous reports" citing the recruitment of children as young as thirteen to fight alongside ISIS. A UN report states, "Witnesses claimed that the majority of ISIL elements patrolling the streets of Mosul were underage children, aged 13 to 16 years." Children have been seen wearing masks over their faces and carrying guns almost as large as their bodies.[9]

Children robbed of their innocence and forced to kill.

JUST AS I was finishing writing this morning, I began reviewing a fresh batch of video from a refugee camp in Northern

Iraq. Almost all of the stories in this book come from first-hand accounts of eyewitnesses of the atrocities of ISIS, and also come from the courageous work of journalists, aid workers, and human rights activists who have risked their lives to try and save the lives of innocent Iraqis and Syrians. On a number of occasions, I've sent researchers into the places harboring thousands of refugees to document and verify facts, and many times we've gathered this documentation on video.

The clip that struck me just now was of a paralyzed little boy. He's blind and he's missing his right hand. I have no idea whether he was born this way or if his disability is a casualty of war. He sits on a rug in the middle of about fifty people. They are listening to him sing.

At first glimpse, I found hope in the video. I saw an innocent child bringing a light-hearted moment to a crowd of desperate people. His voice is beautiful, and the people are cheering for him as he sings.

It caused me to smile.

There's just something amazing about hearing a child sing. There's something touching and powerful about the angelic sound. It was a respite amidst the tear-filled images I had watched over and over in this batch of video—a piece of peace in a sea of pain caused by the hatred, chaos, and abuse of ISIS.

I immediately started digging through notes from the team

that recorded the video that day to find a translation of the little boy's song.

It wasn't what I expected.

My heart was shattered by what I read:

> *Our water spring has been ruined by ISIS.*
> *Mount Sinjar, my homeland.*
> *Today it's deserted and the springs are dry.*
> *Disaster, disaster, disaster today . . . we are witnessing*
>   *a disaster.*
> *Misery, misery, misery.*

Read those words again, read them carefully and slowly, and let the pain of each of them seep deep down into your bones. Muster every ounce of empathy inside of you as you read them again and imagine you're hearing your own child singing these awful words. Don't simply read, but feel them with all the feeling you have inside of you:

> *Our water spring has been ruined by ISIS.*
> *Mount Sinjar, my homeland.*
> *Today it's deserted and the springs are dry.*
> *Disaster, disaster, disaster today . . . we are witnessing*
>   *a disaster.*
> *Misery, misery, misery.*

The little boy's lullaby reminded me of the famous song sung by generations of children called "Ring a Ring o' Roses." Its mysterious lyrics sung half-heartedly by so many children were hewn in the horror of the Great Plague in the United Kingdom. Kids now singing "Ashes, Ashes . . . We all fall down" have no idea the lyrics were inspired by the death of masses at the impersonal hands of a great disease.

Yet, that child's lullaby in Iraq was not inspired by an impersonal enemy, but rather, by a very personal one, a terrifying one that has taken great pleasure in robbing children of their future.

The trauma of the experience of ISIS taking over his home is wedged so deeply into that little boy's heart that he'll never be the same.

Their hatred has stolen his innocence. They have profoundly traumatized him and traumatized his entire generation.

Somehow we are all guilty for letting it happen on our watch.

This is not *his* world. He's too young to do anything about this.

This is our world.

The generation that has allowed ISIS to exist.

And while ISIS exists, no child is safe.

Even our own.

3

ENSLAVE THEIR WIVES AND ABUSE THEIR DAUGHTERS

Really, I wouldn't believe it had I not seen it with my own eyes.

An Arabic-language television channel had obtained a crudely produced video shot last fall during the "slave market" day in ISIS-controlled Mosul.

In the video, ISIS "soldiers" are heard joking about the women they will buy and abuse. If you were imagining this scene you would see a street gang of thugs bragging about their conquests while their eyes shift from side to side betraying the guilty consciences they bear underneath it all.

But it's not that way at all.

These men don't speak shamefully about their debauchery. There's no hint of conscience in the banter between them. On the contrary, there is an arrogant pride that rings clear in their voices as they willingly brag to one another. The video shot on a cell phone records them saying things like:

"Today is distribution day, God-willing . . . each man takes his share."

"I swear man, I am searching for a girl. I hope I find one."

"Today is the day of slaves and we should have our share."

"Where is my Yazidi girl?"

"The price differs if she has blue eyes."

"If she is fifteen years old, I have to check her, check her teeth. If she doesn't have teeth, why would I want her?"[1]

In recent years, the awful phenomenon of human trafficking has received a great deal of attention. Many organizations have begun focusing on it, notable books have been written on the subject, and governments around the world have committed to addressing it. Yet, human trafficking seems to be confined to the recesses of society, hidden in seedy hotels and in the dark underworld where drug traffickers, mafia members, and secret agents do their dealings. Everyone knows it exists, but it seems as separate from us and as far away as another planet. It happens in the shadows.

Yet, in ISIS-controlled Iraq and Syria, there isn't anything hidden about the trafficking of women. There's no sense of morality that pushes its abhorrence underground. On the contrary, it's right out there for all the world to see. The trafficking takes place in broad daylight with women being treated like animals. They are bartered over, sometimes traded, and sometimes discounted. Thousands of innocent women have been kidnapped, as many as seven thousand at a time,[2] and ISIS gives them as rewards to their best fighters or sells them in organized slave markets to raise money for the state. The slave markets even have price lists. One price list smuggled out of the country and published by Iraqi News organized the enslaved women according to age and religion.

Christian and Yazidi girls are particularly targeted and were priced according to age:

- Ages one–nine costs $172
- Ages ten–twenty costs $130
- Ages twenty–thirty costs $86
- Ages thirty–forty costs $75
- Ages forty–fifty costs $43

Below the prices on the document, bearing the official seal of the Islamic State of Iraq, reads, "Customers are allowed to purchase only three items [slaves] with the exception of customers from Turkey, Syria, and Gulf countries. Obey and follow the rules and laws of the Islamic State or be killed."

The top of the price list reads, "We have received news that the demand in the women and cattle market has sharply decreased and that will affect Islamic State revenues as well as the funding of the Mujahideen in the battlefield. Therefore, we have made some changes. Below are the prices for Yazidi and

Christian women [slaves]."³ Women have been reduced to the humiliating term "items." While we are not sure of the entire distorted logic of ISIS in determining their prices, it is clear that they were selling these women at a "discount" based upon the amount of them that were now available. The price list was created in order to enact "price controls" so that the market's supply and demand were properly balanced.

Yazidis, in particular, have borne the brunt of this sustained and horrific abuse. The former Human Rights Minister of Iraq, Mohammed Shia al-Sudani, claims to have evidence of ISIS *burying Yazidi women and children alive in the mass graves* used against their executed husbands and fathers. Minister al-Sudani says that ISIS fighters "cheered and waved their weapons over the corpses" as they committed their "vicious atrocity."⁴

During a particular sustained attack on Mount Sinjar in the fall of 2014, more than five thousand Yazidi men were killed, and as many as seven thousand Yazidi women were captured to serve as slaves and concubines for ISIS fighters. One Yazidi scholar asserted: "In every place where Yazidi women or families are held, jihadists come and randomly select women that they take away."⁵

Then, there's the ISIS magazine, *Dabiq*, which devoted an entire essay to justifying the enslavement of Yazidis. ISIS claims they do so "by the permission of Allah," and in so doing, they are fulfilling a promise Allah made to them. They promise that their practice of slavery will continue for generations, and that their children and grandchildren will sell the sons and daughters of those they capture in future slaves markets.

Particularly chilling is ISIS' justification for reinstituting slavery. They argue that the "desertion of [sexual] slavery had led to an increase in . . . adultery . . . because the [Sharia] alternative to marriage is not available, so a man who cannot afford marriage to a free woman finds himself surrounded by temptation towards sin."[6] They go so far as to say that they are *obligated* to treat non-Muslim women this way. "Taking their women as concubines is a firmly established aspect of the [Sharia law] that if one were to deny or mock, he would be denying the verses of the Qur'an and the narrations of the Prophet."[7] Their "price controls" in the slave market were about ensuring that as many men in the Islamic State had access to as many concubines as possible. It is to ISIS not only their right, but also a necessity.

We interviewed a young mother who told us about the moment ISIS arrived at her home. She is a lovely woman, but the toll on her life is evident. Rarely did she look up and initiate eye contact. She spoke in hushed tones, the pain and embarrassment crystal clear whether one understood her language or not. She told her story as her two young, innocent children were sitting between her and her husband.

Here is what she told us:

They had daggers and swords—they said "shall we start beheading women and children or start with the old and the disabled?" One of them came to me and said, "If you're not a Muslim I'm going to take you and the children and I will kill your husband." I said, "No, we are going to stay Christian. We won't abandon our religion. How can we abandon our religion?" We stayed, and the second day we saw captured girls. Maybe thirty Yazidi girls held by them in a house in Mosul where they sent Christians [too]. At two in the morning we heard girls screaming. The gunmen were raping the girls. You could tell they were being raped. They were hurting them. They were saying "these ones don't have religion. We will behead you all unless you convert to our Islamic religion."

Mayat, a seventeen-year-old Yazidi girl who had been kidnapped by ISIS, told the *Independent* about "rooms of horror" where "women are raped, often by different men and throughout the day." Mayat continued, "They threaten us and beat us if we try to resist. Often I wish they would beat me so hard I will die. But they are cowards even in this. None of them have the courage to end our suffering." She said that her life would remain "forever scarred by the torture" she had received over a few weeks, and that "even if I survive, I don't think I'll be able to remove this horror from my mind. . . . They have already killed my body. They are now killing my soul."[8]

When Kurdish forces retook an area near the Mosul dam from ISIS, a Kurdish soldier "discovered a woman, naked and bound, who had been repeatedly raped." Then, as he went deeper into the neighborhood they discovered "another woman in the same state."[9] The ISIS fighters had been "rewarded" with the opportunity to sexually abuse these captured women.[10] These barbarians were allowed to go from barbarism-to-barbarism, exercising their lust in the name of their god; sex traded for their service in a Holy War. They would fight like animals, and pause only to let their satanic lust run wild on an innocent woman or child. On one occasion, a kidnapped young woman who was being held in a brothel, claimed to have been raped more than thirty times in just a few short hours. Almost nothing is more detestable, and there are thousands of these stories.

Until the arrival of ISIS they were, "little girls, who were going to school and playing with dolls. . . . ISIS' men not only leave behind dead bodies in their wake but also women and children who are scarred for life."[11] In no place on planet earth is it more dangerous to be a woman than in the presence of ISIS.

Just ask Esther, a wide-eyed, olive-skinned, fourteen-year-old girl, who told us about the day the terrorists kidnapped her entire family. They took them from place to place for weeks. Eventually, Esther escaped and ended up in the home of ISIS collaborators. They turned her back over to ISIS who decided to punish her by beating her with a hose and cables. In Esther's own words:

They were saying, "It's useless for you to try to escape because wherever you go they will bring you back." They hit me everywhere—my hands, my legs, my back . . . everyone took a turn, even the children from the village . . . the youngest was five years old, then eight, and thirteen. Then three adults, and they were taking turns for more than an hour. Then, they would rest and come back and beat me some more.

Esther was in the eighth grade when ISIS nearly ended her life. Her favorite subject in school was Arabic, and she still hopes to grow up to become a chemistry teacher. Now, she's free of ISIS, but at the time of my writing she is sitting in a non-winterized tent in the cold north of Iraq and it's the dead of winter. She's hoping she survives this next, great trial as she did her first.

What a tragedy it would be for her to have survived imprisonment by ISIS only to die of the cold! ISIS would win either way.

THEN THERE'S ZENA.

She was twenty years old, studying chemical engineering in Mosul when ISIS came into town. Like so many young women, she had dreams and ambitions. She was not just an average student, but an excellent one and her future was looking bright.

Thankfully, she had come of college age in the slightly more peaceful period between the end of the second Iraq War and the arrival of ISIS. Unlike those a bit older, she saw the sun rising after a long dark night, and there was a glimmer of hope in the sky.

Then ISIS came toward Mosul with their machine guns welded to the top of their pickup trucks, with their stolen UN vehicles and stolen American weapons. They came with brutality, with fury, and with a deep-seated, premodern opinion of the role of women in society.

So, Zena had three strikes against her.

First, she was a Christian.

Second, she was a woman.

Third, she was a woman with ambition.

When I met Zena, she was living in an elementary school that had become a makeshift shelter for hundreds of refugees. It was nearly two months after she had arrived there, and she was still wearing the same pajamas that she was wearing the night she awakened in the middle of the night and forced to flee her home.

When I asked her how she was doing, she told me in a solemn tone, "They took our future."

Then she explained to me how they had arrived in the middle of the night jarring her family from bed, and forcing them to leave with nothing but their lives. ISIS has since taken over their homes and stolen everything from within them. They are petty thieves—arguing that anything owned by an "infidel" is rightfully theirs.

Zena also told me that "they destroyed our church," and she did so immediately after describing how hopeless they all feel. Her sense of hope was tied to the preservation of the Christian community she had grown up in. The destruction of her church, and the other churches in Mosul, was an assault on their security in a deep and personal way.

While ISIS mainly enslaves and sexually abuses Christian and Yazidi women, they treat all women with contempt, and particularly women who have any kind of independence or authority. Zena was among the lucky ones. Most of the time, they simply murder women who dare do anything but tend to the home and children.

In the Syrian city of Al-Mayadin, they captured and beheaded a female dentist because she treated both men and women. Many others have been stoned to death and buried in shallow graves because of "adultery." Some girls as young as thirteen have been kidnapped and forcibly married to ISIS fighters; and all women in ISIS territory are required to follow a strict dress code. Women and girls are not allowed to be in the presence of men outside of their immediate family, and those who break these rules are whipped viciously. Women with no male relatives are particularly vulnerable.[12] In Mosul, among the former candidates for public office who have been publicly executed by ISIS, several were "women who were shot in the head."[13] Before being executed, the women had been detained by ISIS for forty-five days.

One of the first things ISIS did when they took Mosul was imprison or kill any political leader who might oppose them. In and around the village of Sderat, ISIS killed two other women who had run for public office and abducted another. Still another woman was killed by ISIS, near Mosul, after being accused of organizing and participating in a strike. Female doctors in Mosul who have been allowed to continue their practice purely out of necessity have been forced to cover their faces and to dress in all black if they are married. One female doctor was stopped from performing an emergency procedure because her face wasn't properly covered.[14] ISIS has even threatened to "execute male teachers who teach female students."[15]

After reviewing a video taken in the immediate aftermath of the fall of Mosul, a reporter from *The Guardian* noted, "Armed men are hanging off the back of trucks, as the crowd films them. One fighter leans out a car window, wagging his finger. The footage provides a translation. The fighter has spotted a woman and he is ordering her to cover up . . . that fighter had barely arrived in Mosul yet his first order of business gives us a chilling glimpse of a broader strategy, one that targets women with repression and violence."[16] The reporter goes on to cite example after example of the attempts by Islamic extremists to repress women, threatening death if they don't dress according to the standards of the Islamic State. The author refers to it all as a "sexual jihad."[17] There are many reports of women being beaten with sticks for refusing to wear a veil, and many others have been tortured and murdered for everything you can possibly imagine.

When asked why he fled his hometown upon the arrival of ISIS, an elderly man told us, "I will tell why I left my district. I left it because they stormed our house barbarically at 2:00 a.m. harassing us, pointing their flashlights toward our women. We didn't come from another country. We are from an eastern society. We are Iraqis and we are jealous of our honor. So we left it to avoid them because they already threatened to arrest our women. They told my mother that they would arrest her if they couldn't find us."

As a result, he left to protect his mother, his wife, and his daughters.

The land of ISIS has become the most dangerous place in the world for women and girls, especially Christian women.

There is a true war against women raging with unbridled brutality every single day at the hands of ISIS.

It's time that every woman in the world raises her voice to say, "Not on my watch."

For the sake of our daughters, this evil must be utterly destroyed.

4

THE CROSSES
OF ANKAWA

In an Iraqi-Christian village there was a man called Joseph. He is a man of middle age who has the energy of someone half his age. He is usually neatly dressed and clean-shaven, but lately he has taken on a more unkempt look—his clothes wrinkled and his face stubbly from shaving neglect. He has strong arms, a long, lean face, uncombed hair, and kind dark eyes. Most significant to our discussion is his profession. Joseph is a pastor.

When he first heard ISIS was on its way, he went frantically from house to house to warn people that their lives were in danger. Eventually, however, he ran out of time. There were just too many Christians and too few hours left. The roads were crowded from those exiting and it quickly became apparent that not everyone would make it out by the time ISIS made it in.

There was one particular family he knew would probably not make it—a family he loved.

I can't imagine what he felt as he went to their door that day. When he got there, he told the four of them, "When ISIS arrives they will come to your door and they will ask you if you are Christian or Muslim. I would tell them 'I am a follower of Jesus.'"

It was a coy bit of advice, given that Muslims consider Jesus a prophet, but—of course—there was no way around ISIS identifying them as members of Iraq's ancient Christian minority.

ISIS could pick out a Christian from a mile away. They came looking for them, and they would err on the side of taking out another Christian over arguing back and forth with themselves as to how Christian they were.

Joseph—the kind, energetic, frazzled pastor—left them with one final word of advice before dashing off to the next group. "If you choose to not convert," he told them, "then just know it will only hurt for a second. I am praying for you."

ISIS did indeed arrive before they could flee.

That family of four refused to convert.

It only hurt for a second.

Surely God himself was standing in their honor as they entered the gates of Heaven that day . . . together, as a family.

IT HAS ALWAYS been a mystery to me why so many Christians in the West struggle to live for what so many Christians in persecuted countries are willing to die for.

I first encountered this type of dedication to Christ in certain precarious parts of Asia where Christians are routinely beaten, imprisoned, and murdered for their faith. I was always struck by this as I spoke to a person with a bullet wound or a prison number tattooed on their arm, or scars on their back. In almost every circumstance, I realized that the persecution against them had only made their faith stronger, and many of them believe that persecution would eventually cause the church to grow. These are not isolated, anecdotal incidents—I've experienced this so many times in so many places around the world.

I remember one particular pastor in a hostile region of Asia who decided to move in the backyard of extremists who hated Christians. He came to that city to plant a church, and was only in the city for a few hours before the extremists showed up at his door.

They threatened him.

In fact, they told him that if he continued with his plan that they would cut him into tiny little pieces and throw him into a river. The young Indian pastor left terrified and went immediately to meet with his mentor in a neighboring city. He desperately needed advice.

Perplexed, he said, "I don't know what to do. They are going to kill me."

His wise mentor, taking advantage of his age and experience, looked at the young pastor, staring deeply into his eyes and said, "Son, I want to ask you a question. Did Jesus ask you to go to that city?"

Without hesitation the young pastor replied, "Yes, that is the burden he put on my heart."

"Are you sure?" the mentor pressed.

Again, the student replied without pause, "Yes, but they are going to kill me, as they have killed those who've come before me."

The older pastor looked down at his hands, as if to collect his thoughts.

Then he looked up, as if to gain his message from heaven.

Finally he looked straight ahead at his young protégé and said, "My dear boy, go back to that city. They will probably come to you and again threaten you."

He paused for another moment and then added, "But remember that Heaven is better than that place."

Next, they prayed.

Then the older man sent the younger man back.

When I met that young pastor, he had a successful school and a beautiful church, and so many people's lives had been touched by his kindness. He cared for numerous poor people in the city, and he was absolutely fearless.

Sacrifice and martyrdom are deeply rooted in Christian identity and Christian theology. They have been in place since the first century, and they are every bit as relevant today as they were back then. Remember, all but one of Jesus' disciples was martyred, and the story of the early church is as triumphant as it is blood-laden.

While ISIS' "martyrs" die believing that their death will get them to heaven, Christian martyrs believe in a different type of martyrdom. Christians believe that Jesus Christ has already given them an invitation to heaven.

The classic text in Scripture is Ephesians 2:8–9:

> For it is by grace you have been saved, through faith—and this is not from yourselves, it is the gift of God—not by works, so that no one can boast.

Christians don't earn that place by their death, but rather they affirm their love for Jesus in their death. Their deaths are all about Jesus, and not about what they get from God in exchange for it, but about what God has given them in exchange for their lives.

Or as Jesus said in John 15:13:

> Greater love has no one than this: to lay down one's life for one's friends.

Christians are giving their lives, affirming their love for Jesus. Once again they are being forced to pay for their faith with their lives, and once again—as in so many times in history—they are willing to do what is required of them in order to demonstrate to the world that hate is no match for the love of Jesus.

All over Iraq and Syria, we are witnessing the type of faith that most of us only read about in the earliest part of Christian history. We are witnessing an attack on the faithful that has demonstrated time and again that true faith is so deeply rooted in our souls that hell-on-earth can't steal it from us. The Christian church was hewn on the anvil of persecution. It knows that anvil well, and while in this day we are witnessing its evil in rare form—perhaps in a way we've rarely seen it in church history—it is not a new thing, but an old thing.

The brutality of the opposition can only be measured against the defiance of the faith of those they are attempting to kill—that defiance rooted in the very love of Jesus himself.

Take Zena, for instance, the twenty-year-old chemical engineering student I met in Northern Iraq. It didn't take long for me to ascertain that this young woman was bright, and my guess was that she was once happy, engaged in life and filled with the stamina that accompanies youth. In our chat about the pain and suffering she had endured, she took a full ten minutes to lament the horror that she had experienced, and the sense of hopelessness that now gripped her family and her future. I expected her to be so beaten down that even her faith might lie in shambles as well.

So, out of respect, I chose not to ask her about her faith. I knew these would be hard questions in general, but especially difficult questions for her. Questions like: "Where was God when all of this was happening?"

Then, suddenly, I felt a prompting in my heart to ask.

Something was telling me to "go there," and so I did.

I asked her how this experience had affected her faith in Jesus Christ.

The question hung in the air for a second.

I didn't know what was coming, but didn't expect it to be good.

But, to my surprise, her tone changed entirely. The depression and hurt that had monopolized the conversation to this point went away almost entirely. A glimmer came into her eye and her countenance lightened.

A tender defiance filled her voice as she revealed to me her unwavering commitment to Jesus Christ. She didn't say that she doubted God or wondered why God allowed them to suffer so much so often.

Instead she said, "We thank Jesus one thousand times for life."

After all the death she had seen, she appreciated her life so much more. She knew that the air in her lungs was a gift from

God himself, and it was a gift so many of her brothers and sisters hadn't been able to enjoy.

She continued, "Our Lord Jesus saved us from death; maybe this is the beginning of our story."

It reminded me of the words of the apostle Paul written while teaching the church in Corinth about the importance of the resurrection of Jesus Christ. He wrote, "I face death every day."

Yet, as he said to the persecuted church in Rome (the city within which he was eventually beheaded in Romans 8:35–39),

Who shall separate us from the love of Christ? Shall trouble or hardship or persecution or famine or nakedness or danger or sword? As it is written, "For your sake we face death all day long; we are considered as sheep to be slaughtered." No, in all things we are more than conquerors through him who loved us. For I am convinced that neither death nor life, neither angels nor demons, neither the present nor the future, nor any powers, neither height nor depth, nor anything else in all creation, will be able to separate us from the love of God that is in Christ Jesus our Lord.

Amazing, isn't it?

Those words ring very differently read within the context of the assault on Christians in Iraq and Syria.

They are as true today as they were then.

———— ◆ ————

Two thousand years later, evil men are still beheading Christians, and the love of Christ continues to prevail over their hatred.

IT'S INTERESTING THAT nearly every Christian leader we've encountered in this region felt the historic consequence of the persecution they were enduring. Several times I heard people say, "Now, Jesus is requiring us to carry our own crosses," and they referenced the suffering of previous generations.

They knew well the words of Christians from a different era, like Ignatius of Antioch. Antioch is in Syria, and Ignatius was a pupil of the apostle John. Ignatius became a martyr fed to wild beasts at the hands of the Romans. It was a fate he thought to be inevitable, and so much so that he defiantly taunted it in his own writings:

> May I enjoy the wild beasts that are prepared for me; and I pray that they may be found eager to rush upon me, which also I will entice to devour me . . . If they be unwilling to assail me, I will compel them to do so. . . . Now I begin to be a disciple, and have no desire after anything visible or invisible, that I may attain to Jesus Christ. Let fire and the cross; let the crowds of wild beasts; let breakings, tearings, and

———

separations of bones; let cutting off of members, let bruising to pieces of the whole body; and let the very torment of the devil come upon me; only let me attain to Jesus Christ.[2]

This sense of defiance and commitment to Jesus is very much alive in the Middle East among these Christian populations. Like Tertullian, the Christian author who lived in North Africa in the third century, they believe that "the blood of the martyrs is the seed of the church," and that "the Christian, even when he is condemned, gives thanks."

So, through their excruciating pain, through the weight of their trauma, and their thousand kinds of brokenness, they don't resent the call to suffer that God has put upon their shoulders, but they welcome it. They celebrate it, and they feel honored by it. They inspire us by it.

No one exemplified this more than the Archbishop of Mosul, whom I mentioned earlier.

He told me that shortly after ISIS arrived in his city, they decided to destroy the ancient tomb of the prophet Jonah. Both Christians and Muslims had celebrated this shrine to Jonah for hundreds of years. They made pilgrimages there, and prayed there. Since the fourteenth century, a mosque has sat upon that site where Christian churches had previously been for hundreds of years before.

The extreme version of Islam adhered to by ISIS doesn't

allow for any shrine to anyone, and so they decided to blow it up. In doing so, they annihilated a site revered for thousands of years by two religions, including the one they claim.

When the archbishop was telling me this story, that same glimmer appeared in his eye that I had seen in Zena's eyes only a few days before. He explained to me that in destroying the Mosque to Jonah, ISIS had inadvertently uncovered the ruins of an ancient Byzantine church that they didn't even know existed.

In ISIS' attempt to wipe the meaning of that site from the face of the earth, they had accidently revealed once again the biblical admonition that "the gates of hell shall not prevail against [the church]" (Matthew 16:18 KJV).

The archbishop found great pleasure in the inability of ISIS to wipe from their hearts what they had tried to wipe from the face of the earth.

Then there's Sister Rose, a young nun from Mosul, who has poured her life into the lives of Christian refugees as they have fled from city to city, and she among them.

She had paid particular attention to refugees that no one else cared for. She sought out those who weren't in refugee camps and that hadn't found help from international institutions. She went searching for them in fields and abandoned buildings, and found those sleeping on sidewalks and wandering aimlessly down roads to nowhere. She had experienced enough trauma herself to have every bit of an excuse to not tend to anyone's wounds but her own. Yet, she was a nun who was called by God to care for the poor, and despite having only ten minutes to leave her home when ISIS arrived, she hadn't for a moment thought about herself. She piled people into trucks as ISIS drove through the city in ambulances, disguised as paramedics. She warned others and fought to help them escape. She witnessed a man her age being shot in the head, and women pleading with her to take their children so ISIS wouldn't sell, kill, or abuse them.

She pressed on, helping others, despite the horror erupting around her and the pain welling up inside of her.

The plan was to drive to a city an hour away, but the massive caravan of refugees heading in the same direction took more than nine hours to arrive. All along the way, they had no food or water. Sister Rose pushed aside her own suffering to comfort those who had suffered more. She had only the clothes on her back when she fled, but at least she had her life and she believed her life was left with her in order to give life to others. Till this day, she hasn't stopped caring for those displaced. Her abundant love floods those broken streets in defiance of ISIS.

I'll never forget what she told us when we met with her: "I lived in America. Americans are wonderful people. It's shocking to me that they are so silent in the face of our genocide. Please help us. Raise your voice for us. Our children are dying. In America you care for your pets so well, can you care for your Christian brothers and sisters who are suffering?"[3]

———◆———

I saw this sense of commitment to faith and love again and again as I learned more and more about the suffering church in Iraq and Syria. It was crystal clear that every attempt by ISIS to suppress their faith had only galvanized it. The hatred of ISIS had only made them love more, and in every refugee camp I saw men, women, and children praying—praying earnestly.

I saw makeshift churches set up in tents, and nuns, priests, and pastors with sweat on their brow. Sister Rose was one of many who were giving every part of themselves as Jesus had given every part of himself. I'm convinced that these men and women will be welcomed to heaven with a celebration like we can't even comprehend. They are the nameless, faceless servants who have shown us what true love really is, in a world so void of it. They have given it without any credit, and without any reward. They have done it because it's the right thing to do and because they love God as he first loved them.

Their faith is the best of faith, and in the words of my very good friend and the cochairman of the World Economic Forum's Global Agenda Council on the Role of Faith, Dr. Chris Seiple, it is always the "best of faith [that] defeats the worst of religion."[4]

THE MOMENT I arrived in Iraq last fall, I asked if we could go immediately to visit the tented villages that had been set up

———

all over the city. Almost all of those living within these areas are Christian families from Mosul and Qaraqosh.

The conditions were awful, but at least those living there were alive.

These people weren't living in tents made for refugees. They were living in makeshift tents pieced together as best as they could. They weren't waterproof or winterized, and the conditions were just impossible. These families were only in the conditions they were living in because of their faith. It was their commitment to Jesus that had threatened their lives. Had they been willing to convert to ISIS' version of Islam, they would still be in their homes, and still be living in their cities. Instead, they were living in tents—tents that flood easily and that stood an inevitable defeat against the harshness of an Iraqi winter.

What struck me the most about the tents was not their awful condition, but the crosses accompanying them. One in particular caught my eye, so I went directly to it. At the entrance of the tent, the family had placed a large cross that reached high into the sky.

It's that cross that nearly got them killed.

It's that cross that cost them their home and their livelihood, and—almost certainly—the life of someone they loved.

That cross was a burden that they had to bear, and they had every reason in the world to shield themselves from it.

Yet, the first thing they did when they set up their tent was to make sure everyone knew they still loved that cross, and that ISIS knew exactly where to find them should they come after them again.

The crosses of Ankawa—on their tents, tattooed on their arms, and hanging around their necks—have never been so prominent, and to them, they have never been so important.

In fact, one family snuck back into their village—which had been annihilated by ISIS—and under the cover of night they crawled atop their ancient church and affixed again the cross that ISIS had torn down.

For hell itself is not enough to pressure them to deny that cross.

They will raise it high, and bear it even if it costs them their own lives.

They remain perplexed why so many Christians are barely willing to live for what they are so willing to die for.

PART TWO

WHY ISIS MATTERS
TO YOU

5

ISIS *IS* IN YOUR BACKYARD

Reaching heights of fame, achieving stellar success, or exhibiting the greatness of a honed and trained talent—these are things that make any person remarkable. I work every day with remarkable people just like that. But one of the most remarkable people I've met in recent years had none of those achievements. His is a life that straddles two worlds. In one, he loves his parents and usually shows up to exchange gifts at Christmas with the family. But his professional life is so secretive that neither family nor friend knows what he does. Typically, his mother and father don't even know where he is.

Sitting over a cup of coffee with this man would have looked as normal from the outside as a chat among friends. No one in the coffee shop would have thought anything of us.

Yet this man has lived, for most of the last ten years, behind enemy lines. He has befriended and fought terrorism from the inside. As a result, he knew things that most Americans could never imagine. He spoke languages that most Western people have never heard, or even knew existed.

His was the life of the terrorist. He had been trained to think like a terrorist. Because of that, he could spot one. When he met a potential threat for the first time, he could assess immediately whether the ISIS-inspired person was actually capable of doing the terrorist acts the person professed to desire to carry out. He was the type of person who knew exactly what to do if a bomb went off in a café, and he was trained to defend himself with almost nothing against almost anyone. He was a chameleon who could adapt to different circumstances. You could be talking to him one day and have no idea that you had talked to him the previous day. He could look and act entirely different in the blink of an eye.

By the time we sat down for that cup of coffee, this man had saved countless lives by risking his own. He had been as close to the most terrifying people on earth as he was to me across the table. He is one of the only people on earth to have breathed the same air without being one of them.

Much of what this hero could have said was classified information. The information he shared had to be sketchy. But one overriding theme he came back to again and again, one thing he drove into my mind that still haunts me, was this:

ISIS is in more places than you think . . . they are already here.

At one point, he said, in essence, "ISIS is capable of more than you believe, and when you least expect them, they are most likely nearby."

This is not a passing threat or propagandist. ISIS represents a group of people who share the same ideology that results in only one goal: TO KILL YOU.

They have no conscience. They are rarely deterred. They are patient to wait until the right time. And they don't mind taking themselves out if that's what is required to take you out.

That's the cold, hard truth. Truth sets us free.

ISIS-INSPIRED PEOPLE ARE IN YOUR CITY

What is also true is that ISIS cells and ISIS-inspired people are right on your doorstep. ISIS doesn't need a geographical region to have a base of operations. Their base is right inside your own computer, just a click away. They are exercising a stateless war conducted by non-state actors who are missionaries to their cause. These "missionaries" can show up anytime, in anyplace. These ISIS-inspired people don't have to be a member of a club to be inspired to violence and murder in the name of their ideology.

Imagine landing a good-paying job in a community just outside the largest city in your state. The city is ripped by an EF5 tornado, the highest possible tornado rating, but you and your family survive unscathed. Even your job remains intact at the local food processing plant. When you survived the tornado, you felt you'd dodged a bullet and started thinking about the important things in life. Now you look forward to working another eight years or so, and then retiring to do the things you've always wanted to do.

What you don't know is that by the time of the tornado, another killer has been feeding on ISIS rhetoric for six months. After you survive the killer tornado, another four months go by. Then one day, you walk into work as usual. Soon, there is commotion and confusion. A person you recognize as a former coworker approaches you with a knife. The next thing your coworkers know, your head is on the ground as the murderer takes your life by beheading.

That's exactly what happened to Colleen Hufford at her job outside Oklahoma City in September 2014. Her attacker had spent time watching beheadings online. He didn't have a club membership, but he was every bit a part of the fabric of ISIS.

In the largest city in Australia, workers were attacked by another radical while working in a place of children's fantasies— a chocolate café. A gunman named Man Haron Monis locked the doors during morning rush hour on December 15, 2014, and held ten customers and eight employees hostage. His headband read, "We are ready to sacrifice for you, O Muhammad." He also forced them to hold up a black ISIS-type flag in the windows.

Police cordoned off a section of downtown Sydney, and emptied the Sydney Opera House for sixteen hours, until they were able to storm the café and bring the crisis to an end. The shop manager, Tori Johnson, was murdered when he tried to wrestle the gun from the killer. Also killed was a mother of three, attorney Katrina Dawson. She was meeting a colleague for coffee that morning.

While law enforcement and the media initially tried not to label the attack as ISIS-inspired, they eventually labeled it terrorism. Some media outlets have scoffed at the idea that it was not ISIS-inspired.[1]

What do these stories have in common? These ISIS-inspired terrorists were recruited and trained via the Internet. Here are five reasons these reports are both terrifying and important for you and me.

1. Inspiration and Instruction Are Readily Available

The tools that we have created in the West to foster communication, accelerate innovation, and advance learning are the very same tools that ISIS is actively using to try and destroy us.

You use the Internet—and so do the people inspired by ISIS in your city.

- You use it to find recipes; ISIS uses it to find recipes *for bombs.*
- You use it to watch funny videos; ISIS uses it to post videos *of beheadings.*
- You use it to connect with friends; ISIS uses it to *radicalize cobelligerents.*
- You use it to watch inspirational sermons and messages; ISIS uses it to listen to *diatribes* by the late Anwar al-Awlaki and Osama bin Laden.
- You use it as a dating site—and *they do too.*[2]

In a city like yours, in a neighborhood like yours, in a house like yours—

- Right now, someone is listening to a hate-filled sermon *in English* by Anwar al-Awlaki.
- Right now, someone is chatting on the Internet with other disaffected and simmering radicals.
- Right now, someone is posting the incendiary words, memes, and posts of ISIS on their social media accounts, and "liking" those of their friends.
- Right now, someone near you is reading about how to make a bomb or blow up an airplane.

And while most of these people may never act out, it only takes one, and that one may be next door. The Internet is flooded with terrorist propaganda; Google recently announced that YouTube is so overloaded with such content that their expansive censoring division is incapable of keeping up.[3] In one study of Arabic language tweets about ISIS organized by country, researchers determined that 21.4 percent of all Arabic tweets in the United States related to ISIS were in support of the Islamic State. It was 23.8 percent in the United Kingdom, 20.8 percent in France, 47.6 pecent in Qatar, 22.2 percent in Turkey, and 31 percent in Belgium.

Only 19.8 percent of Arabic language tweets in Saudi Arabia were in support of ISIS, less than the United States, France, and the United Kingdom.[4]

2. Individuals Can Now Do What Only Nation States Could Previously Do

Abraham Lincoln famously declared in 1838:

At what point shall we expect the approach of danger? By what means shall we fortify against it?—Shall we expect some transatlantic military giant, to step the Ocean, and crush us at a blow? Never!—All the armies of Europe, Asia and Africa combined, with all the treasure of the earth (our own excepted) in their military chest; with a Buonaparte for a commander, could not by force, take a drink from the Ohio, or make a track on the Blue Ridge, in a trial of a thousand years.[5]

Unfortunately, the world looks very different today

- . . . after 9/11 in New York, Washington D.C., and Pennsylvania
- . . . after 7/7 in London
- . . . after 3/11 in Madrid
- . . . after 1/7 in Paris
- . . . after 12/15 in Sydney

The truth of the matter is individuals can now do what only nation states could do a generation ago. The sneak attack on Pearl Harbor required 353 aircraft, six heavy aircraft carriers, and twenty-four additional support vessels, killing more than twenty-five hundred people.[6] By contrast, the 9/11 attacks on United States soil were carried out by nineteen militants, and killed nearly three thousand people.[7] Just think about it—there weren't enough 9/11 terrorists to even put one on each of the support ships in Pearl Harbor. Let alone, the aircraft carriers. Let alone, the aircraft—and still the 9/11 terrorists caused greater loss of life.

And while Al-Qaeda terrorized the world with its sophisticated, coordinated, and audacious attacks, ISIS has not only fielded armies (something Al-Qaeda never achieved) and established governments, it has also inspired and equipped *individuals* to commit acts of terror. They have done so not only in the Middle East, but also in middle America, Canada, and Europe. Individuals whose only connection to ISIS is a shared allegiance to an *idea*, and access to the Internet.

In the meantime, ISIS has drawn the West into costly airstrikes while a second front is outsourced to cobelligerents around the world. The airstrikes by the United States, and its allies, against Kobani cost $8.2 million a day during the four months it took for the West to wrestle a non-strategic town of forty-five thousand people from ISIS.

We are fighting a different kind of war trying to use a strategy from another time, thinking the sophistication of our own weapons can protect us.

In the meantime, terrorism experts describe ISIS' global jihad as a "leaderless resistance—in which self-proclaimed combatants are linked by common beliefs and goals and wage a common terrorist war, but operate autonomously."[8] These are individuals who didn't travel to some training camp in Yemen or Sudan, weren't born in Baghdad or the Panjshir Valley, but rather were born in the West, radicalized in the West, and emboldened to commit individual acts of terror in the West. They needn't be embedded because they have grown up among us. They can be recruited, educated, and inspired by those in Syria while they sit at their laptops in Nebraska. Educated only with the instructions they can find on the Internet, and armed only with everyday materials that can be easily attained in any metropolitan area, these individuals are determined to strike a blow at the individuals, installations, and institutions around them. Because they were raised among us many of them have traveled under American and European passports. Take, for example, Jihadi John who spoke with a perfect British accent as he threatened to behead—and eventually beheaded— journalists like James Foley and Kenji Goto, or the jihadist who beheaded twenty-one Coptic Christians in Libya in February 2015. Linguists identified his accent as clearly American or Canadian. Could he have an American passport? Could he live in your hometown?

It only takes one.

- Consider the underreported attempt by a suicide bomber on our nation's capital. A twenty-nine-year-old party DJ was arrested for attempting to kill U.S. government officials. Amine el Khalifi was caught on video as part of an FBI sting. Agents even videotaped him purchasing nails in a Home Depot to use as shrapnel in his suicide vest. He was arrested on February 12, 2012, two blocks from the U.S. Capitol, with what he thought was a suicide vest that he picked up from an abandoned warehouse. The suicide vest was a fake given to him by undercover FBI agents. Had he been working with others, his mission would have been successful. He is serving thirty years in jail. When given his sentence, he said, "I just want to say that I love Allah."

- In broad daylight on the afternoon of October 23, 2014, an ISIS-inspired man attacked four Queens, New York, police officers with a hatchet. Police Commissioner Bill Bratton called it a "terrorist attack, certainly." He added that walking the streets of New York with an axe indicated some preparation. A search of the man's computer revealed ISIS sites he'd visited and the propaganda that radicalized him.[9]

- On January 14, 2015, a twenty-year-old Ohio man was arrested for plans to blow up the U.S. Capitol and kill government officials. Like most of these attackers, he had been posting ISIS-inspired threats on the Internet to "wage jihad." Christopher Cornell was picked up after purchasing two semiautomatic weapons and six hundred rounds of ammunition at a local gun shop.

3. ISIS Isn't Just "Over There"—They're *Right Here*

ISIS "members" can pop up anywhere. So, where are they and how can we see them? While no rational person would claim that all Muslims are adherents to ISIS ideology, generally, followers of ISIS ideology identify themselves as Muslims.

Islam is the fastest-growing religion in Europe.[10] The saturation of Islam in the West has been steadily increasing, almost entirely through immigration and childbirth, as opposed to conversion. It is on the rise in most other places as well:

- In the United States, 0.8 percent of the population is Muslim.
- In Canada, 2.8 percent of the population is Muslim.
- In the United Kingdom, 4.6 percent of the population is Muslim.
- In Germany, 5 percent of the population is Muslim.
- In France, 7.5 percent of the population is Muslim.[11]
- In some countries, like the United States, members of Islam are well integrated. Its members serve in Congress, in the foreign service, and in the U.S. military, fighting to preserve U.S. freedoms and American values—including the freedom to worship as we choose. In Canada, the integration is even more complete.

And yet, there is no clear path to radicalization. The attacker in Oklahoma City was a former Christian who "converted" to ISIS ideology. Images of the Canadian attacker, whose father was Libyan, gripped the world as he stormed the parliament building and made it almost all the way to the prime minister before being stopped on October 22, 2014.

No one knows why Michael Zehaf-Bibeau followed a "radicalization process." He applied for a passport to Syria before launching his attack in Ottawa. First, he shot to death a soldier at the National War Memorial, then raced through the halls of Parliament.[12]

Another Canadian man from Quebec, Martin Rouleau, had run down two Canadian soldiers two days earlier. He was also killed by police, giving him the status of "martyr."

And yet another Canadian man, earlier that month in Toronto, was discovered before he could carry out a "knife and gun" attack in a public place. Authorities believe such attacks are planned in public places in part so police will arrive to kill the attacker and provide him or her with the "martyr" status.

In Europe, it's a different story. Members of Islam in the United Kingdom, France, Germany, and the Low Countries tend to suffer from high rates of unemployment and poverty and a low level of assimilation, perhaps due to discrimination.[13] The problem is that a lack of assimilation breeds a feeling of alienation, and alienation sometimes results in radicalization. "The root problem—where ideological extremism flourishes—is alienation. Disaffected, second- and third-generation immigrant youth are seeking alternative communities of belonging that conflict with a free society."[14] In countries where immigrants are fully integrated, the second or third generation tends to blend indistinguishably from the host culture. But in this case, we see the exact opposite. They burrow into their identity, living in a third culture, and looking for an outlet for their frustration with their disenfranchisement.

Most recently, the radicalization of these types of young people have captured the attention of the world, and their victims have moved the hearts of most of the seven billion people sharing our planet.

In Paris, on Wednesday, January 7, 2015, gunmen and brothers, Chérif and Saïd Kouachi, stormed the offices of the satirical magazine *Charlie Hebdo*, killing twelve employees of the publication. As they raced away, the driver doubled back on the street and one of the attackers also shot a police officer, injuring him. The world watched in horror as video footage then showed one of the gunmen walking up to the injured officer and shooting him dead at close range.

Witnesses at the magazine headquarters told reporters that the attackers shouted, "We have avenged the prophet Muhammad" and "God is great" in Arabic. The men were apprehended two days later and killed. They had already told the media that they wanted to be killed and die as "martyrs."

On the day of the *Charlie Hebdo* killings, a jogger was killed by a gunman in a park. The next day, another gunman killed a police officer and shot a bystander. And the next day, a gunman took hostages at a kosher supermarket in Paris. That standoff resulted in four hostages being killed, and the gunman also being killed—making him yet another "martyr."

On January 15, 2015, in Belgium, a "sleeper cell" of ISIS was raided by police, killing two of them. Many more are on the loose, and authorities believe there could be as many as twenty other cells with hundreds of trained assassins prepared to carry out attacks. The two members killed had both fought in Syria before returning to Belgium to bring their war home.

This was all too familiar for Belgians. In May of the previous year, an attack on the Jewish Museum in Brussels left four dead. Police apprehended Medhi Nemmouche, who had fought with ISIS extremists in Syria for more than a year.

In both the New World and the Old World, in the East and in the West, in the developing world and developed world, radicalized immigrants and "homegrown" terrorists alike are committing acts of violence in the name of Islam. And these days, there are many more around us. Imagine what exists underground? What I've referenced here are only those incidences which have risen to the surface. They are the tip of the iceberg, and you've probably forgotten now that all of this has happened. Sadly—soberingly—the worst is probably yet to come.

JONAH

Nineveh was a bad place in which to hang out back in the old days. It certainly wasn't a place that we would consider receptive to the message of the prophet, Jonah. Yet, that is exactly where the Lord called the prophet to preach.

There were, however, glimmers of light in an otherwise dark history of this city. One scholar pulls back the historical curtain for us:

" . . . during the reign of Adad-nirari III (810–783 BC) there was a swing toward monotheism, which may have been the result of Jonah's preaching. The awakening may have occurred in the days of Ashur-dan III (771–734 BC). The plague of 765, the eclipse of the sun in 763 BC, and a second plague in 759 BC were events of the type regarded by ancients as evidence of divine judgment, and could have prepared the people to receive Jonah's message."[15]

You likely know the rest of the story. After Jonah tried to hide on the cruise ship to Spain, after the great fish swallowed him up and then spit him out, Jonah reprogrammed his GPS to march right into Nineveh to preach the Good News. The result? One of the greatest spiritual revivals in history!

The King of Nineveh declared, "Let men call on God earnestly that each may turn from his wicked way and from the violence which is in his hands. Who knows, God may turn and relent, and withdraw His burning anger so that we shall not perish." (Jonah 3:8–9 NASB)

Imagine the scene: believers in the Lord, right there in downtown Mosul in Northern Iraq, thousands of years ago.

4. The Idea of the "Caliphate" Resonates with Many Extremists

The caliphate was "the political-religious state comprising the Muslim community and the lands and peoples under its dominion"[16] which developed in the centuries following the death of Muhammad. "Caliph," the term for the ruler of the caliphate, means "successor" in Arabic. In other words, the caliphate was Muhammad's successor as the ruler of the Islamic world. But more than just an Arabic word vaguely synonymous with "Kingdom," the important thing is what "caliphate" symbolizes for these Muslims, namely a Golden Age of Islam.

- **Greatness.** As Professor Hugh Kennedy notes, "Seventy years after [Muhammad's] death, this Muslim world stretched from Spain and Morocco right the way to

Central Asia and to the southern bits of Pakistan, so a huge empire that was all . . . under the control of a single Muslim leader."[17]

- **Unity and achievement**. A time of prosperity and leadership in commerce, mathematics, science, and the classics.
- **Enlightened and popularly chosen leadership**. Reza Pankhurst argues that the caliph was to be "the choice of the people . . . appointed in order to be responsible to them, apply Islamic law and ensure it's executed." He adds that the true caliph "is not above the law."[18]

So when Abu Bakr al-Baghdadi declared himself the Caliph of all Muslims, he was calling himself the successor to Muhammad, demanding allegiance from Muslims, and calling them to conquest.

"IS has skilfully exploited the elements in the caliphate's history which best serve its purposes. The historian Hugh Kennedy has pointed out, for example, that their black uniforms and flags deliberately echo the black robes the Abbasids adopted as their court dress in the 8th Century, thus recalling Islam's Golden Age. And their original title—the Islamic State of Iraq and the Levant—harks back to the days when there was no national border between the two countries, because both territories were part of the great Islamic caliphate."[19]

Nearly all of the Muslim world rejected Abu Bakr al-Baghdadi's claim to restore the caliphate—but not all of them. Indeed, at a minimum, two thousand people from the West have made their way to Syria to fight for ISIS.[20] Holly Yan cites these reasons:

1. ISIS preys on a recruit's sense of identity;
2. ISIS appeals to their religious duty;
3. ISIS operates a sophisticated propaganda machine;
4. It exerts a cult-like control;
5. It uses its successes as a tool.[21]

It's bad enough that Westerners are going to fight for ISIS, but the scariest part is that some are coming back—trained, radicalized, and with the ability to blend in—and some of them arriving via their United States passport. U.S. Senator John McCain, a former soldier and prisoner of war, has drawn attention to this trend. He said to a CNN reporter, "[Airstrikes are] simply a very narrow and focused approach to a problem which is metastasizing as we speak. There was a guy a month ago that was in Syria, went back to the United States, came back and blew himself up. We're tracking 100 Americans who are over there now fighting for ISIS. ISIS is attracting extreme elements from all over the world, much less the Arab world. And what have we done?"

McCain was speaking about Moner Mohammad Abu-Salha, a Florida native who grew up in the posh city of Vero Beach, Florida. He was trained in Syria, then returned to the U.S. Later, he returned to Syria and was successful in a suicide bombing in Syria.

A naturalized American citizen was charged for facilitating recruitment for Al-Qaeda. He pled guilty in July 2014 and awaits trial as this is written.

How do these people freely travel the world and have access in all levels of society among all peoples?

5. They Are Using Sophisticated Tools

The first bombing of the World Trade Center in 1993 was in many ways a comedy of errors. "The terrorists intended to send the North Tower (Tower 1) crashing into the South Tower (Tower 2), bringing both towers down and killing thousands of people."[22] As it was, six people died, and more than a thousand were injured.[23] In the 1997 HBO docudrama of the events, *Path to Paradise: The Untold Story of the World Trade Center Bombing*, the terrorists are portrayed as bumbling idiots who were too stupid to execute their plans or cover their tracks. A number of the 9/11 plotters were part of this attack, and it's safe to say that they learned the lessons, and applied them with a vengeance just eight years later.

In just the same way, the masterminds of ISIS have learned the lessons:

- Their generals have learned the lessons of war, fighting the Syrian army to stalemate, and chasing the decimated Iraqi army to the outskirts of Baghdad with a rapidity and lethality shocking to even the most-experienced military analysts. Along the way, they are seizing and holding land, and accumulating sophisticated weaponry abandoned by retreating soldiers. As the Kurdish interior minister told a delegation I was a part of to Iraqi Kurdistan, "We are using old Soviet weapons to fight ISIS with their stolen weapons from the United States."
- Their propagandists have learned the lessons of the war of ideas, producing video, web, and printed materials that are sophisticated, designed to make an emotional connection, and everything is highly-produced.
- Their accountants lead "the best financed group we've ever seen," according to Matthew Levitt, director of the Stein Program on Counterterrorism and Intelligence at the Washington Institute for Near East Policy.[24] In late 2014, ISIS was making between $1 million and

$4 million a day off the proceeds of smuggled oil, and another $20 million last year in ransom money.[25]

In other words, if you think we have nothing to fear, think again.

But while you are thinking, think also about how we can eradicate the threat. What can a Christian sitting in a church in Ogallala, Nebraska, or Duluth, Georgia, do about ISIS?

In 1976, the Ebola virus was identified in the Democratic Republic of Congo near the Ebola River. On September 26, 2014, a Liberian national, Thomas Eric Duncan, went to a hospital emergency room in Dallas. Two days later, he was hospitalized. Two days after that, the Center for Disease Control announced he had Ebola. A little more than a week later, Duncan was dead.

By then, two nurses who helped Duncan, Amber Joy Vinson and Nina Pham, contracted the disease. For weeks, the national spotlight was on the brave Americans fighting the disease, and the terrible reasons the disease had spread. Every broadcast and news article alternated between cheers and jeers for those fighting it, and those thought responsible for it.

Within months, after Vinson and Pham were declared healthy, thousands of workers had descended on West Africa to fight the outbreak. Pop-up hospitals appeared. Doctors, nurses, and aid workers were covered head to toe to protect themselves from the disease. Within months, due to nationwide efforts, Nigeria and Senegal were declared Ebola-free. A surge of medical workers kept flooding into Liberia, Guinea, and Sierra Leone.

What happened? The U.S. rallied to fight a deadly disease once the threat came to our shores. Health workers, politicians, researchers, and scientists all concluded that to keep Americans safe at home, we would have to fight the disease outside our borders.

Diseases can kill, and words also have the power to kill. The radical words and influence of ISIS that is resulting in genocide, mass killings, rampant rape, and decapitations in other countries are not staying in those countries. They've already been exported, and they've landed in your neighborhood, and possibly right in the device on which you are reading this book.

It's time Americans recognize the threat to our freedom, and it's long past time for American Christians to take action. Chapter 6 explains how we can do just that.

And we can't wait around expecting someone else to care. ISIS is a grassroots movement, and it requires a grassroots response.

6

HOW WE DEFEAT ISIS

You know, I totally get it.

I know why people aren't that engaged in caring for the Christians—and others—whose lives are being threatened by ISIS.

It's not that they don't care *about* them, it's that they don't care *for* them, and the reason why is because it's hard to invest your time, money, and energy in a cause so distant from you, so confined to the other side of the world, and so irrelevant to your everyday life. We're all caught up in our normal lives. We're taking care of our families and taking care of our jobs, and trying to squeeze some meaning into the ounce of free time we have remaining after all the other things competing for our attention. It's just hard to turn our eyes to Iraq or Syria when there's so little of our attention to go around in the first place. Not to mention, this particular part of the world seems plague-ridden, and it has received—in the views of many—"enough" time, attention, and money from the West.

But, if nothing else is apparent from what you've read thus far, it should be apparent that ISIS is a very real threat to our very real lives, and we simply don't have the luxury of being disengaged from this crisis. This isn't a crisis "confined" to another part of the world. It's anything but confined. It's running wildly all over planet earth, and it's growing at a rate that ought to cause us all to shudder.

This global phenomenon will only be successfully addressed by a truly global response. It's a grassroots movement that will only be checked by a different kind of grassroots movement. And—as I alluded to earlier—when the world gets fed up with something (like Ebola), it reacts fiercely, decisively, and comprehensively. Around dinner tables families discuss the issue, everyone gives a little money to someone working on the cause, churches and community organizations rally others to it, and there's a certain sense of personal responsibility at the heart of it all because we have a very real belief in the potential personal repercussions.

In this case, as a Christian, this is particularly poignant for *me*.

For while the ISIS crisis weaves its harmful and consequential effects into many aspects of our society, its threat to my "brothers and sisters" in Christ is a family affair.

They are going after my family, and they are going after them in a particularly insulting place—the very place where our devotion was born.

We really have no option.

We must raise our voices.

We must rush to help.

EDUCATE YOURSELVES

The lack of concern for this crisis isn't for a lack of information. In fact, the war in Syria that preceded the current crisis represented the first time in history when regular people's cell phone videos and images made them ad hoc journalists, recording the play-by-play of the conflict erupting around them. Their photos and videos were uploaded onto YouTube, Facebook, and Twitter, and the world was flooded with real-time updates from those caught in the cross fire.

All of this was subsidized by a nearly unprecedented amount of traditional and freelance journalists whose courageous reporting floods the Internet. In fact, you could argue that there is a secondary war going on in the region. It's an information war, raging between the ISIS propaganda machine and the journalists whose reporting has forced the hand of Western governments.

Nearly half of the journalists murdered in the world in 2014 were killed in Syria or Iraq.

Dozens have been captured, imprisoned, or killed. The majority of those Westerners executed by ISIS have been journalists or aid workers, and almost all of them put themselves in unusual peril in order to tell us the story of what's happening there.

While some of what I've written about in this book has come from my own experience on the ground or through sources not accessible to everyone, there are plenty of stories here that I learned only from reading the news. We're living in a world where one can educate oneself about almost anything, and it's essential that we do it. On Twitter, for example, I follow journalists who are covering Iraq and Syria for major international news networks. I also frequent the websites of Al Jazeera, France 24, BBC, Rudaw, and Iraqi News. They are all in English, and you can get a very good understanding of what's happening firsthand by what you read there.

You should be reading from these sources, as well, to educate yourself so you can speak with understanding and with authority to others who might care if they knew.

Additionally, so many Western Christians are from Protestant and Evangelical traditions, where we have a tendency to discount the contributions of Catholic and Orthodox communities in the preservation of our faith in the Middle

East. We must educate ourselves on these communities; get to know their stories and their leaders. Read books about them and expose yourselves to their history and their current circumstances.

Because of a relatively small group of Christians who educated themselves and cared enough to raise their voices between October and December of 2014, more than seventy-two thousand ISIS-affected refugees survived winter.[1] It all began with taking the time to learn; and what they learned forced them to do as much as they could as quickly as they could.

GIVE TO THOSE PRESERVING AND REBUILDING SOCIETY

Then, you should provide practical assistance to those on the ground who are working hard to rescue those in harm's way and to restore those whose lives have been destroyed by ISIS. I was personally involved in the founding of an amazing effort—on behalf of a Hollywood couple, the President of the Institute for Global Engagement, and a number of international leaders—to provide near and long-term support to these communities. We established The Cradle Fund, which you can read about in the back of this book. But there are many other amazing organizations doing significant things to provide lifesaving help to those who have survived ISIS, but now risk their families dying for lack of food or shelter.

I've personally been involved in the amazing work of World Help, The Foundation for Relief and Reconciliation in the Middle East, The Knights of Columbus, the Assyrian Aid Society, the International Orthodox Christian Charities, the Preemptive Love Coalition, the Dominican Sisters of St. Catherine of Siena, and Heart4Lebanon.

The fact is, it takes enormous resources from around the world to preserve the lives of those displaced. In a world of two billion professing Christians, it's a shame that we haven't done a better job of caring for the few hundred thousand who have been displaced by ISIS. We have more than the means if we had the will to do something significant. We ought to be caring for these people in the way that we hope someone would be caring for us.

And we mustn't expect governments to take care of the problem. In particular, Christian communities have never found it acceptable to outsource their kindness to governments, but they have always accepted responsibility to deliver their kindness on behalf of Jesus directly to those who are in harm's way. Governments inevitably calculate their decisions according to numerous geopolitical concerns. Governments are rarely fast, rarely efficient, and rarely thorough. They almost always engage too late, and seldom work with objectivity. Governments ought to be batting cleanup for the Christians, and other religious communities around the world, who are commanded by their faith to step into crises with compassion.

DON'T UNDERESTIMATE OR OVERSIMPLIFY THE CRISIS

Too often, people fail to understand the complexity of global issues. They come to conclusions, misinterpret what they observe or hear, and can sometimes exacerbate the problem by their uneducated approach or their lack of humility or understanding. This is not a book about the intricacies of this geopolitical crisis. Maybe one day I'll write that book, but when I do, it will be much longer than this one, for the complexity of the politics of that region of the world is dizzying. It intersects with myriad issues related to the most persistent conflicts of our time—of all time. In order to understand why Iraq and Syria have become safe havens for terrorists, and in order to discover the solution, you must have a thorough handle on the politics of at least the United States, the United Kingdom, France, Germany, Iran, Iraq, Israel, Jordan, Lebanon, Russia, Bosnia, Saudi Arabia, Syria, Yemen, and the list goes on and on. These are not easy questions, and there are not easy solutions. Just as soon as you think you've come to a conclusion, you ought to immediately become skeptical of your newfound confidence. For—as I would often tell my students—"everything is always more complicated than it seems."

This is no more apparent than in the rhetoric used by some Christians when referencing Islam, Muslims, or Muslim countries. They pile ISIS onto a global faith adhered to by many millions of wonderful people—people who condemn ISIS as much as Christians do, and people who make our world a better place by their benevolence and generosity. The fact is that the Muslim community around the world has suffered the most at the hands of these radicals. Far more Muslims have died than Christians, and many of those Christians, and other affected ethnic and religious communities that have survived, have only survived because of the efforts of Islamic leaders in the region.

ISIS will only be defeated, and that region of the world will only be stabilized, through the cooperation of Eastern and Western countries, and through the collaboration of Christian, Jewish, and Muslim leaders. When Christians raise their voices with incendiary rhetoric, they not only demonstrate their lack of understanding, they alienate the very people who are more than willing to align themselves with us in order to address that which threatens us all and which we can only solve together.

Seek to understand before you speak as if you understand.

Seek to work with those who believe as you even though they embrace a faith different than your own.

DANIEL

One of the most significant events in the history of Israel is known as the Exile. As much as the Hebrews loved their land of Palestine, how painful it must have been to be forced to leave home and go into a foreign land enslaved.

Included in this mass evacuation of their homeland is the young man named Daniel. Famous for his withstanding the Lion's Den and the Fiery Furnace with his three companions, Shadrach, Meschach and Abednego, Daniel found his new home to be what today we would call Babylon, Iraq.

A short lesson on a long period of history is in order to fully understand and appreciate the context surrounding the Book of Daniel. Here we have an excellent summary:

The Chaldeans, a Semitic people, were living in south-eastern Babylonia about 1000 BC. They were an aggressive and nomadic people who were troublesome to the Babylonians. One of their leaders, Merodachbaladan later ascended the throne and ruled Babylon in the eighth century BC. Assyria, under Sennacherib, destroyed Babylon because of its rebelliousness, but the city was later restored by Esarhaddon. In 626 BC Nabolpolassar, a Chaldean, rebelled against

Assyria and established the new Babylonian Empire. In 612, together with Cyaxares the Mede and the king of the Scythians, he destroyed the city of Nineveh. In 605 the Neo-Babylonian Empire was challenged by the Egyptians under the leadership of Pharoah Necho, but the forces of Egypt were decisively defeated in the Battle of Carchemish, by Nabopolassar's son and successor, Nebuchadnezzar (605–562). Jehoiakim, whom Necho had placed upon the throne of Judah (II Kings 23:34), became the vassal of Nebuchadnezzar (II Kings 24:1) who now occupied Palestine, deporting hostages of noble blood to Babylon in 605, among whom were Daniel and his three companions (Daniel 1:1–7).[2]

Even though the Exile is considered a difficult time, we also know the important principle that God does some of his best work in the midst of tough circumstances. Like gold coming through the process of the Refiner's fire, Daniel is a rich and powerful example of one of those men whose faith was only made stronger in the furnace. Here we are, all these thousands of years later, still inspired by his willingness to shine bright amid persecution for his belief.

And he is best known for his time in Iraq.

BEFRIEND THE OTHER

We must also reach out to those communities that have the potential to facilitate radicalism.

One of the great tragedies of our time is that despite living in an enormously diverse world, we rarely know the names, stories, and beliefs of those who are different than us. This lack of relationship allows us to come to conclusions about one another, and when incubated in poverty, disenfranchisement, or under the influence of a compelling and harmful teacher, it can cause enormous harm to society. People are not born terrorists. They are made to be terrorists by a wicked brew of circumstances that normally involves poverty or disenfranchisement of some kind, coupled with the powerful ideological influence of a teacher or mentor, and a misunderstanding of "the other."

It's no coincidence that radicalism metastasizes within disenfranchised communities and the poor immigrant communities of the West—where hopelessness draws them to a desperate search for meaning in sometimes dangerous places. Many of those who eventually find radicalism could have found another path, a more hopeful path. But once they find themselves on a path of hatred, it's nearly impossible to break free from its grip. Only love kills hate, and proactive love hedges against hate. Put differently, and as I put it previously, "It is the best of faith that defeats the worst of religion."

It has never been more important to get to know others who are different than you. The truth is that most ISIS sympathizers have never had a meaningful interaction with a Christian before. They've never been the recipient of Christian kindness or generosity. Their misguided perspective of Christianity isn't unlike the perspective that some Christians have of Islam, for it's much easier to hate those you've never met. And many of those who hate Christianity come to their hatred having never benefited from the best of our faith. They package our faith within the context of our country's politics and assume that Christianity is synonymous with all kinds of things, except the one thing that we ought to be synonymous with—love.

It has never been more important for Christians to love and serve their communities, and to demonstrate their true faith in the heart of those places where an inaccurate perspective of their faith exists. For centuries, Christians cared for their communities. One particularly anti-Christian official in the Roman Empire once remarked that "the godless Galileans care for our poor and their own."[3]

From the very beginning, Christians were known in their communities as those who brought light into darkness, and cared for people in need—especially the "other," whoever the "other" was.

Somehow, we seem to have lost our sense of self, and rather than flooding the world with our abundant love, we've left our faith to get rebranded and abused and misinterpreted and taken advantage of.

Jesus gave us good advice that has never been more needed than it is today, "They will know that we are Christians by our love" (see John 13:35).

The fact is that in much of the Middle East these ancient Christian communities coexisted with Islam for centuries, precisely because they were known to be friends of all, enemies of none, and filled with love and kindness.

Whether or not you believe war was justified, the unmistakable fact is that over the last twenty years, increasing military engagement in the region by Western powers has caused a rebranding of Christianity in the Middle East—allowing radical Muslims to be able to define Western war as a new crusade of Christian countries against Islamic ones.

They've taken advantage of it all and built a narrative that is being embraced all over the region. The reputation of love that persisted for centuries in these Christian communities has been replaced with an accusation of holy war.

Never before has it been more important for those who claim to represent the love of Jesus to love in superabundant form. We must do so among those different from us *here*, and we must do so among those different from us *there*.

Every act of love is a dagger in the heart of ISIS.

May they bleed to death.

PART THREE

———— ✦ ————

WHAT WE ARE
LOSING

7

IRAQ—THE LAND
OF THE BIBLE

Recently, a friend and I were having lunch and a typically light conversation discussing family, friends, jobs, health, politics, and sports. At one point, however, the subject changed by me making the comment, "Tell me some of the highlights in your life over the past few months."

My friend didn't pause a moment before answering, "That's an easy one, Johnnie. My wife and I traveled to the Holy Land just a few months ago. Neither of us had ever been there before, so needless to say, it was the classic 'once in a lifetime,' eye-opening experience."

I smiled and nodded, remembering my first visit to the region. So many trips to that special locale have taken place since that first one, but the rush of walking where Jesus walked came back to me like a cool breeze on a warm day.

"Tell me about some of the places you visited and the sites that you saw," I encouraged.

"Of course," he replied. My friend willingly shared happy memories about his bus excursions to Jericho, Capernaum, Nazareth, Caesarea Philippi, Jerusalem, and of course, Bethlehem, the place where Jesus was born.

He caught me off guard with his next comment. "One of the high points of the trip took place in a gift shop in Bethlehem," my friend volunteered.

"Really?" I replied, a bit mystified at what could possibly happen at a store that would be considered a high point in comparison to the biblical sites my friend was seeing. In fact, I hardly go into those stores because of the haggling and commercialism. It somehow spoils everything for me. I love Bethlehem, and have met with a remarkable Catholic woman who serves as the mayor of the city. I know the president of the city's Bible college, but the gift shops?

"We took the bus from Jerusalem to Bethlehem and at one point in the tour, our guide told the bus driver to stop and allow us to go into this one particular gift shop right there in downtown Bethlehem. The guide explained to us that he was a friend with the owner and that, as a result, there would be a 'deep discount' for items purchased.

"After all our souvenir needs had been met, our guide said to us, 'Ladies and gentlemen, you may be interested to know that my friend, the owner, knows how to speak the ancient language of Aramaic. I'm sure you are aware that Aramaic was the language Jesus spoke when he was here on earth. How many would like to hear our friend say a few words in that language?'

"Of course we all raised our hands and nodded in eager agreement. The shop owner became very solemn and invited us to bow our heads. He brought chills to our spines as he spoke aloud The Lord's Prayer in the language Jesus first used to communicate it all those years ago."

He paused for a moment before adding, "Johnnie, there's just something about that language."

It caused me to remember my own first time hearing The Lord's Prayer prayed in Aramaic. I was with a patriarch of the Orthodox church based in Damascus. We had spent two days discussing the plight of their communities in Iraq and Syria, as well as Egypt and Lebanon, and then as an aside in the middle of such intense conversation, the patriarch decided to pray. So, that was how he prayed and the language within which he prayed it.

From Jesus' very lips to my ears, the words spoken as Jesus spoke them; I almost lose composure writing about it.

Very few people in the world still speak that language and pray that prayer in the same way, but nearly all of them live in the path of ISIS, and many of them have already been killed.

I share this story with you in order to introduce an important subject—the history of the Assyrian Empire.

What does one have to do with the other?

Is there really a connection?

Yes. It is because of Assyria that the language of Jesus in Palestine was the language called Aramaic; and it was because of the Assyrians that that language has been preserved till this very day.

Ancient Assyria is modern Iraq.

THE HISTORY OF ASSYRIA

The history of the Eastern Church, in large part, is framed by the history of Assyria.

If you've read the Old Testament, you will remember there are quite a few references to Assyria, especially among the prophets. Assyria and Babylonia are often spoken of, and usually occupy the role of the villain in the text. Many of us grew up thinking of Assyria and Babylonia as the same place, but they are not. Assyria was to the north and Babylonia to the south, but both were located in modern Iraq:

Assyria is one of the ancient kingdoms of Mesopotamia.

While Babylonia, the southern kingdom, occupied the plain

between Baghdad and the Persian Gulf, Assyria was generally bounded on the west by the Syrian Desert, on the south by Babylonia and on the north and east by the Armenian and Persian hills. "Assyria" was also used to refer to the Assyrian empire which reached its zenith in the 8th and 7th Centuries B.C. and included Babylonia, Elam, Media, Syria, Palestine and Arabia, along with South Anatolia, Cilicia and Egypt . . .

. . . Politically, power oscillated back and forth between Assyria and Babylonia, Assyria being generally the leading power, especially in the period 900–600 B.C. This is the period in which Assyria figures prominently as an invader and oppressor in the Biblical narrative and in the Bible.[1]

The Assyrians controlled and connected the world that preceded Jesus in a way that made Jesus' arrival and the communication of his message possible. It's not an exaggeration to say that without the influence of the Assyrians—even before they converted to Christianity—the church would not have grown as it has.[2]

When my friend at lunch made the passing comment, "Johnnie, there's just something about that language," he had no idea how profound his observation was.

The Assyrians created and championed the Aramaic language that Jesus himself spoke and that was the popular dialect among those living in Jesus' time. It's not just the language of Jesus that makes Assyria relevant to our Christian heritage. So much of the Bible hinges upon this great—now Iraqi—land as Dr. Kenneth Boa, a noted Biblical scholar, points out:

> The conversion of the Ninevites in response to Jonah's message of judgment took place about 760 BC. The revival was evidently short-lived, because the Assyrians soon returned to their ruthless practices. In 722 BC Sargon II of Assyria destroyed Samaria, the capital of the northern kingdom of Israel, and scattered the ten tribes. Led by Sennacherib, the Assyrians also came close to capturing Jerusalem in the reign of King Hezekiah in 701 BC. By the time of Nahum (c. 660 BC), Assyria reached the peak of its prosperity and power under Ashurbanipal (669–633 BC). This King extended Assyria's influence farther than had any of his predecessors. Nineveh became the mightiest city on earth.[3]

God knew the role Nineveh would play in history only a few generations earlier when he sent Jonah to preach on his behalf in that city. Jonah planted a seed of truth in that city.

In a description that appears to be part fairy tale and part action movie script (yet, it's all true!), history accurately records the strength of the Assyrian capital of Nineveh with accounts of walls around the city that were so thick three chariots could ride side by side by side on their tops. If high, deep walls weren't enough, the city was surrounded by a moat one-hundred-and-fifty feet wide and sixty feet deep.

That sounds pretty close to impenetrable, if you ask me. However, returning to the Old Testament book of Nahum, the prophet foretold of the city's utter destruction. Realistically, how could something like that happen to such a strong city? Boa fills in the details for us:

> Assyrian power faded under Ashurbanipal's sons, Ashuretlilani (633–629 BC) and Sinsharishkun (629–612 BC). Nahum predicted that Nineveh would end "with an overflowing flood" (Nahum 1:8), and this is precisely what occurred. The Tigris River overflowed its banks and the flood destroyed part of Nineveh's wall. The Babylonians invaded through this breach in the wall, plundered the city and set it on fire.[4]

Interestingly, God has always had a place for Iraq in the story he was writing with history. It was here that Adam and Eve were created, it was from here Abraham was sent, and it was here where prophets like Jonah and Nahum preached. Then Israel was taken captive by the Assyrians which, while being a terrible ordeal, simultaneously resulted in the preservation of so much of the Old Testament text and culture. For the Israelis were allowed to live within the Assyrian Empire as exiles, as opposed to being entirely eliminated as so many defeated peoples had been before them. God has always had a place for Iraq in his story.

EZEKIEL

A biblical prophet wandered the streets of Iraq. Most likely a contemporary with Daniel, this prophet also lived while Nebuchadnezzar was the king on the throne. At thirty years of age, Ezekiel was instructed by God to write his book to the exiled Judeans in Babylon.

> The Book of Ezekiel was written during the time of Judah's bondage to Babylon under Nebuchadnezzar's rule. Ezekiel lived with a group of captives in Tel Aviv (not the modern-day city by that name), located beside the Kebar River (Ezekiel 3:15) in Babylon. The exact settlement is unknown, but the Kebar River has been identified with the Grand Canal in Babylon. The canal branched off from the Euphrates just above Babylon and flowed east of the city. It continued through the site of ancient Nippur and then reentered the Euphrates near Uruk (biblical Erech).[5]

God gave this thirty-year-old young man a twofold message to pass along to the exiles in Iraq. He explained to them that they lost their homeland because they were unfaithful to God and since he is a holy, righteous God, he was required to discipline them for their wayward behavior. Secondly, however, the book is filled with the hope that they will one day be united with the land of their birth. There is always hope despite the persecution, there is always another chapter to the story, a land to return to, a victory in the waiting.

While in Iraq, Ezekiel's redundant message from God is perfectly clear. "The people will know that I am God," he states. That phrase appears no less than sixty-three times in the book. It's the one thing he wanted them to know, and the one thing every Christian I know embraces in modern Iraq. In their suffering or in their prosperity, in their peace or in the middle of war, they know—and the world will know—that God is with them.

Eventually, the preaching of generations of prophets paid off. The persistence of God's plan for premodern Iraq prevailed for after the arrival, death, and resurrection of Jesus Christ, tradition holds that the apostle Thomas—the disciple who gained the popular nickname "Doubting Thomas"—took the gospel eastward into the Assyrian boundaries, then known simply as Syria.[6]

Tradition teaches that Thomas was responsible for the church in Syria that would become known as the Syriac Orthodox Church. Throughout the centuries that followed, that church continued to grow and prosper, and perhaps the most unlikely of all people converted entirely to Christianity. The same fierce warriors who were known for impaling or beheading of those they captured became preachers of the love of Jesus. Those Jonah and Nahum preached to became those who would go on to preach to others. The Assyrians became Christians, and to this day, nearly every one of them identifies as Christian.

Nina Shea, director of the Hudson Institute's Center for Religious Freedom, has noted that:

> The Nineveh area is profoundly significant to Iraq's Christians. From antiquity, it has been the homeland of the Assyrians, who accepted Christianity, according to tradition, from St. Thomas the Apostle, himself. It is studded with historic churches and monasteries, some dating from the 4th century, like Mar Mattai of the Syriac Orthodox Church. Christianity spread from this region by Syriac missionaries across Asia to Tibet, China, and Mongolia . . . Western Christians also owe an immense spiritual, theological and cultural debt to this Church. Iraq's Christians still pray in Aramaic, the language of Jesus.[7]

Did you catch the historical chain in her paragraph?

We start with the apostle Thomas and move forward a few centuries to the Mar Mattai monastery that dates back to the fourth century. It's that link to the monastery that caught my attention, because as we fast-forward again several centuries, we see that Mar Mattai is once again in the news.

Christianity Today reported earlier in 2014:

> Several sources in mainly Christian areas have confirmed that militants have entered their villages too. A local Christian reports that ISIS extremists are now in control of a well-known "Christian" village in Qaraqosh, where the guards ran away. Another Christian declared that ISIS militants also entered the Mar Behnam Monastery. Some 200 families, many Christian, are now hosted at the Mar Mattai Monastery.[8]

Current-day Christians—our living and breathing brothers and sisters in Christ Jesus—were living in Mar Mattai, that monastery that dates back sixteen hundred years. The tapestry known as the church continues to weave her story through the generations, using a place like Mar Mattai as a common thread. History is not just the world of stuffy old stories in dusty old books. Mar Mattai's contribution to history is much broader than just Christian history, as Yale historian Joel S. Baden has written:

Mar Mattai . . . became one of the most important Christian monasteries by the eighth century, and was particularly renowned for its library. . . .

It is likely that Syriac monks were partly responsible for the preservation of Greek philosophical, medical and scientific texts by translating them into Syriac and Arabic. A ninth-century Syriac patriarch . . . wrote that the best Syriac manuscripts of Greek writers were to be found at Mar Mattai.[9]

History reminds us that the contribution of Christianity spreads far beyond its community. A thriving Christian community is a blessing to the entire world.

Iraq and Christianity, up until our very modern time, have been inseparable. We are witnessing the rooting out of two thousand years of history, and—make no mistake—the world will be worse for it.

How is it that in our modern world we can actually be wondering whether we are witnessing the extinction of Christianity from Iraq? For many centuries, such a thought would have been utterly incomprehensible.

Today, it might be inevitable.

8

SOME HISTORY YOU MAY NOT HAVE BEEN TAUGHT

There was once a great pagan empire within which Christianity arose. In every corner of its borders, churches began to be planted as Christians settled there and were converted in major cities. The pagan empire grew wary of these followers of Jesus Christ and, therefore, tried to destroy them entirely, and with every attempt the church grew explosively. They multiplied exponentially. Every crucifixion, stoning, imprisonment, beheading, boiling, impaling, and torture only strengthened their resolve and added credibility to their movement.[1]

These Christians were wise and they chose to capitalize on the empire's strengths, utilizing them to spread their message from one corner to the next. The empire built roads, so they planted churches along the roads. The empire shared a common language, so they communicated their message in it. Rivers, seas, and oceans were much more significant back then, and this empire included ports whereby they could be connected with much of their modern world.

But over time, the empire died and faded away, though it left an outline in the form of those churches. When you see a map of those churches you see a map of the Ancient Empire. Perhaps by now you have concluded in your mind the empire I have been describing.[2]

Ready for the surprise?

I'm not writing about the *Roman Empire*.

I'm writing about the *Persian Empire*.

It's an empire that stretched from the Mediterranean Sea to Pakistan, and deep into Central Asia, even sharing a border with China.

It's the Eastern Christian Empire, not the Christianized Roman Empire. What was "pagan" became Christian and then it became "Muslim."

Actually, most of the Muslim world was once the Christian world, and so much of its ancient history is built upon a Christian foundation.

Yet, so many of these Christian communities, and their influence, have faded away into history. The once "Christian" parts of the world are considered "unreached" by missionary enterprises, and the history of these communities is almost entirely unknown.

Christianity in these places faded away as we're watching it fade away in our own time; and at one point, it was an unimaginable fate for a faith that held so much of society together.

History is repeating itself.

Most of us have been taught that Christianity was birthed in Jerusalem, grew westward to Greece, then Rome, and into the countries of Spain, France, and England. We have also been taught that by the Middle Ages, Christianity was mainly European, until it hopped the Atlantic and became American. The heart of Christianity has always been westward.

At least that's what they told us, right?

What many of us fail to realize is that Christianity also moved east as it moved west.

Dr. Phillip Jenkins, whose words I summarized at the beginning of this chapter, adds some very important geographical context to our story of Eastern Christianity:

The Mediterranean world had its very familiar routes, but so did the lands east and northeast of Jerusalem, through Syria, Mesopotamia, and beyond. Still, in early Christian times, travelers could follow sections of the ancient Persian Royal Road, which ran from southwestern Iran through Babylon and into northern Mesopotamia. These were the Asian worlds subjected by Alexander the Great, and they were littered with place-names commemorating him and his generals—all the Alexandrias, Antiochs and Seleucias that stretch as far east as Afghanistan: Kandahar takes its name from Alexander. Through the Middle Ages, Eastern Christians even continued to use a calendar based on the Seleucid Era. Instead of dating events from the birth of Christ, their point of reference was still the establishment of Seleucid rule in Syria/Palestine in 312/311 BC.[3]

As another example, there's a city called Merv in modern Turkmenistan near the Afghan border that was one of the greatest cities on the planet for one thousand years. In fact, in the twelfth century it was the largest city on the planet. Today it is only an archeological site. But for hundreds of years it was the seat of the greatest center of learning anywhere! It had no intellectual peer in Europe. Merv was a city filled with Christians and Christian scholars known for their translating of Scriptures from Greek, Syriac, and Coptic, into the Eastern languages, such as Chinese.

Merv was one of many cities that sat on the busy path known as the Silk Road. That thoroughfare was the capital of world trade and the center of the global economy for a millennium, producing most of the world's wealth. The Silk Road stretched from Antioch through Iraq, Central Asia, and China.

It's not how we've been taught, but when you think of the

heart of Christianity in AD 700 or AD 900, don't think of the Rhine, France, Germany, or England. Think of it this way: if Christianity is currently a little over two thousand years old, then at the halfway mark there were as many Christians in Asia as in Europe! The non-Christian world was once the Christian world.

NAHUM

Nahum's entire writing focused on the city of Nineveh in Northern Iraq, now known as Mosul. Not much is known about Nahum, other than he came from a town called Elkosh. The location of that town is fodder for all manner of biblical speculation, and the scholars have a great time attempting to pin down its coordinates.

But Nahum's message is easy to identify. Nineveh cannot get away with its atrocities indefinitely. There will be a time of great judgment ahead, so the Judeans in exile can take hope and comfort in that message.

To gain the proper context for Nahum's message, consider this summary:

When Nahum prophesied, Assyria was at the height of its power. Having subdued its neighbors, the nation had extended its power into Palestine and distant Egypt. Ashurbanipal's wars were numerous and characterized by ruthlessness and cruelty. He boasted of his violence and shameful atrocities, which included among other things the tearing off of the limbs of his victims, putting out their eyes, impaling them, boiling them in tar, skinning them alive. Assyria prided itself on its cruel and violent atrocities, the number of its corpses and the pyramids of human heads left behind as monuments to its destruction.[4]

That should help us better understand why God had Nahum come down so strongly on Nineveh. Drilling down deeper, read the bragging gloat of one king of Assyria, Ashurnasirpal II, who ruled from 883 BC to 859 BC:

I stormed the mountain peaks and took them. In the midst of the mighty mountain I slaughtered them; with their blood I dyed the mountain red like wool . . . The heads of their warriors I cut off, and I formed them into a pillar over against their city; their young men and their maidens I burned in the fire.[5]

Nahum's message of hope?

Look, there on the mountains, the feet of one who brings good news, who proclaims peace! Celebrate your festivals, Judah, and fulfill your vows. No more will the wicked invade you; they will be completely destroyed. (Nahum 1:15).

"It's tough in Iraq right now," Nahum empathizes.
But someday it will be better.
The good will win.
God will win.

THIS IS THE EASTERN CHURCH

Without question, the finest work done on the study of the Eastern Church is at the hands of Jenkins in his already classic book, *The Lost History of Christianity*. Its subtitle is *The Thousand Year Golden Age of the Church in the Middle East, Africa, and Asia—and How It Died*, from which I've already quoted liberally. He writes in the first pages of the book:

Christianity originated in the Near East, and during the first few centuries it had its greatest centers, its most prestigious churches and monasteries, in Syria, Palestine and Mesopotamia. Early Eastern Christians wrote and thought in Syriac, a language closely related to the Aramaic of Jesus and his apostles.[6]

Moving ahead to the seventh century, Jenkins provides the following conclusion:

> By the time of the Arab conquests of the seventh century, the Jacobites probably held the loyalty of most Christians in greater Syria, while the Nestorians dominated the eastern lands, in what we now call Iraq and Iran.[7]

The "Nazarenes" or "Nestorians" who traced their lineage directly to the apostles, called Jesus "Yeshua" because of their connection to Christianity's heritage. Most likely, Christianity made it to the Pacific before the Atlantic because of the Nestorians. In fact, for many years Christianity fared better in the East than it did in the West! Samarkand was a center of Christianity before most European churches even existed, for instance.

Eastern Christians were at the heart of Christianity from the days of the apostles until at least the 1300s—the first two thirds of Christian history. They spoke Syriac, which was closer to Aramaic, and acted as a conduit of ideas between the East and the West.

They were the scholars of the East, and many of the great contributions to society attributed to Islamic nations happened at the hands of the Christians living within them, and even when Christianity declined in prominence it remained as a presence. In every one of these countries, until our very modern era, there were Christian communities who could trace their lineage for a thousand years.

THE STORY OF TIMOTHY

Not only were there Christian communities in the East, they were thriving Christian communities with powerful and influential leaders. Take, for example, the story of Timothy. In his day, he was the most powerful Christian on earth. Perhaps the best way to help us understand the significance of the growth of the church worldwide is to invite you to pretend with me that we are listening to a newscast from centuries ago.

The time period was approximately AD 800.

First, let's look at the lead story from the West.[8]

It all centers around a man named Charlemagne. Crowned the King of the Franks in AD 771, his kingdom included present-day Belgium, France, Luxembourg, the Netherlands, and Western Germany. One source uses two sentences to sum up his mission and strategy:

He embarked on a mission to unite all Germanic peoples into one kingdom, and [forcibly] convert his subjects to Christianity. A skilled military strategist, he spent much of his reign engaged in warfare in order to accomplish his goals.[9]

It could sound noble, but it wasn't. He was forcibly converting Germans by having priests up river consecrating the river and then having his army chase converts through the area, "converting them." In AD 782, he apparently executed forty-five hundred of them who wouldn't convert. That's the antiquated news in the West.

Now let's turn our attention to the East.

The head of the Eastern Church was a patriarch called Timothy, who lived in the Christian Capital of the World—Baghdad!

Here's his story:

About 780, the bishop Timothy became patriarch, or catholicos of the Church of the East, which was then based at the ancient Mesopotamian city of Seleucia. He . . . lived well into his nineties, dying in 823, and in that long life Timothy devoted himself to spiritual quests as enthusiastically as Charlemagne did to building his worldly empire . . . Timothy was arguably the most significant Christian spiritual leader of his day . . . Perhaps a quarter of the world's Christians looked to Timothy as both spiritual and political head.[10]

We know a great deal about this man Timothy because of his correspondence. He once wrote that in Jericho people had discovered ancient jars with ancient scrolls in them (an early discovery of the Dead Sea Scrolls). To this very day, scholars are conducting careful examinations and study of these scrolls, trying to determine which version of the Old Testament they are most like.

Back then, Timothy dealt masterfully and expertly with these texts when European Christians wouldn't have any clue what to do with them.

Another example in his writings is when he mentions, "It's been a busy year, I've appointed one bishop for the Turks, who are living near a lake in Siberia, and another for the Tibetans."

Did you catch that?

Christianity reached Tibet round about the same time as Buddhism.

At that point "Chang'an" was the capital of China, and it also had a thriving Christian population. In fact, an Indian Buddhist missionary, named Prajna, arrived in the city around AD 800 with a large group of Buddhist Shutras [texts]. The only problem was that they weren't in Chinese.

The solution?

He asked the local Christian bishop to translate them for him!
Why did he ask the bishop?

Because in that time period, in that great Chinese city, the only institution in the city with the intellectual capacity and linguistic expertise to do so was the church. Later, historians believe, those translated documents made it to Japan and became the foundation for Buddhism in Japan.

Christianity in the East was every bit as influential, if not more so, than Christianity in the West. It was certainly more advanced and more sophisticated.

In fact, even during the rise of the Islamic Era, Christians represented the scholars, bureaucrats, and administrators of the Muslim empire!

Jenkins writes:

". . . long after the coming of Islam, rich Christian cultures continued to develop and flourish across the Near East and Asia, with their own distinct literature, art, liturgy, devotion and philosophy."[11]

Understanding the depth and width of the church in the East certainly gives us pause when we evaluate our own Western prejudices of the church. There would be no church in the West had there not been church in the East. Christianity is not just a westward phenomenon. It is only global because it was first Eastern.

IN OUR TIME, we are watching a once-in-a-thousand-year crisis erupt against Christianity in the East. As the head of the Coptic Orthodox Church of England said recently, "We haven't seen this since the atrocities of Genghis Khan in the thirteenth century."

It is medieval and it is awful and it is a threat to our entire civilization. As Dr. Chris Seiple has noted, "To lose the presence of Christians in the birthplace of Christianity is to accelerate instability, while losing precious insight about how best to work in the region."[12]

Despite the threat to civilization presented by ISIS, and despite the threat to our own brothers and sisters in faith, the world has remained largely silent.

Nearly every Christian I know fails to realize and react to the historic significance of what's happening in the Middle East. Could it be that a Christian genocide there is well under way? Could it be that in our modern era we are allowing the destruction of Christianity in the place of its birth? Christianity will have survived innumerable threats by premodern enemies only to be squashed in our modern times under the watchful eye of a world equipped with all it needs to stop the massacre.

The silence is criminal.

Recently, I was struck by the words of one of those who isn't silent.

The Archbishop of Washington, D.C., Cardinal Donald Wuerl, took the opportunity to address the issue at the conclusion of his opening address to the Catholic University of America in August 2014.

He said,

> We cannot in conscience ignore [this]. Often we are asked how is it possible in human history that atrocities occur? They occur for two reasons: there are those prepared to commit them and those who remain silent. The actions in Iraq and Syria today, what's happening to women, children, and men . . . their displacement is the least of the things happening to them . . . is something that we are really not free to ignore.

In that packed convocation, Cardinal Wuerl pleaded with those students, faculty, and staff to do something, all of them, and to do it now, for "sometimes all we have to raise is our voice. I don't want to have it on my conscience that I was complicit in something as horrendous as this, simply for being quiet."

Uncharacteristically, he raised his soft-spoken tone to a pitch so full that it echoed across the cathedral:

Where are the voices? Why a silence? I think each one of us has at least the power to raise our voice. In solidarity with these people distant from us, unknown to us . . . atrocities happen because there are those who commit them and those who simply remain silent.[13]

As for me . . .

I am done being silent.

I will not have it on my conscience that I stood by while two thousand years of Christianity was eliminated from the Middle East.

What about you?

ORGANIZATIONS
I SUPPORT

WORLD HELP

I was introduced to the crisis in Syria by World Help. I serve on the Board of Trustees of World Help, and my wife and I have long been faithful supporters of the organization. We appreciate the work World Help does in many nations around the world. I've seen it firsthand in some of our planet's most complicated places.

They have been working extensively in war-torn communities in the Middle East for many years, and have been actively distributing life-saving provisions to refugees since the very beginning of the conflict in Syria in 2011. World Help facilitated my first visit with Syrian refugees.

They have provided humanitarian assistance to many thousands over the course of this Syrian conflict and other conflicts in the region. Its founder, Dr. Vernon Brewer, is a great man and personal hero and mentor of mine who has literally changed the world in his lifetime.

I would encourage you to learn more and give generously to World Help by visiting: www.worldhelp.net/Iraq. You might also call 434-525-4657 or write to PO Box 501, Forest, VA 24551.

THE CRADLE OF CHRISTIANITY FUND

I am an advisor to, and a founder of, The Cradle Fund, whose mission is to rescue, restore, and return displaced Christians, and others, in the Middle East.

We do so through carefully vetted, local organizations and churches actively at work in the region. The Cradle Fund is a kind of clearinghouse that insures donations are deployed strategically and responsibly with near- and long-term solutions in mind. We are providing immediate humanitarian assistance, but we are also focused on developing a stable future for the entire region.

Our work is being conducted at the invitation of a number of local and regional Christian and Muslims leaders who serve as a leader of their religious community or a leader of their nation, including a head of state.

The Cradle Fund is administered by the Institute for Global Engagement (IGE) and is chaired by Dr. Chris Seiple, who serves as chairman of IGE, as an advisor to the State Department, and is the cochairman of the World Economic Forum's Global Council on the Role of Faith.

Visit www.cradlefund.org *or* www.globalengage.org.
Call: 703-527-3100. *E-mail:* info@globalengage.org.
Write: PO BOX 12205, Arlington, VA 22219-2205.

NOTES

Introduction
1. John Foxe, *Foxe's Book of Martyrs* (repr., Alachua, FL: Bridge Logos Publishers, 2001), 1.
2. Song of Solomon 8:6 CEV.

Chapter 1
1. Johnnie Moore, "We Must Stand Up for Middle East's Persecuted Christians," FoxNews.com, February 3, 2014, http://www.foxnews.com/opinion/2014/01/31/must-stand-up-for-middle-east-persecuted-christians/.
2. Jane Arraf, "Baghdad's Church Victims Buried," PRI, November 5, 2010, http://www.pri.org/stories/2010-11-05/baghdads-church-victims-buried.
3. Ibid.
4. Martin Chulov, "Isis Fighters Surround Syrian Airbase in Rapid Drive to Recapture Lost Territory," August 22, 2014, *Guardian*, http://www.theguardian.com/world/2014/aug/22/isis-syria-airbase-tabqa.
5. Patrick Cockburn, "War with Isis: Islamic Militants Have Army of 200,000, Claims Senior Krudish Leader," *Independent*, November 16, 2014, http://www.independent.co.uk/news/world/middle-east/

war-with-isis-islamic-militants-have-army-of-200000-claims-kurdish-leader-9863418.html.

6. Polly Mosendz, "How Much Does ISIS Make on Selling Oil?" *Newsweek*, November 10, 2104, http://www.newsweek.com/isis-islamic-state-baiji-iraq-syria-oil-283524.

7. Nina Shea, "Where Do Mosul's Christians Go Now? American Help Is Needed," Hudson Institute, June 17, 2014, http://www.hudson.org/research/10377-where-do-mosul-s-christians-go-now-american-help-is-needed.

8. Damien McElroy, "Rome Will Be Conquered Next, Says Leader of 'Islamic State,'" *Telegraph, July 1, 2014, http://www.telegraph.co.uk/news/worldnews/middleeast/syria/10939235/Rome-will-be-conquered-next-says-leader-of-Islamic-State.html.*

9. Ian Black, "Islamic State Leader Bachdadi Reportedly Resurfaces After Claims US Strike Killed Him," Guardian, November 13, 2014, http://www.theguardian.com/world/2014/nov/13/islamic-state-audio-tape-baghdadi.

10. Haider Ala Hamoudi, "A Translation of the ISIS Declaration Expelling the Christians of Mosul," muslimlawprof. org, July 20, 2014, http://muslimlawprof.org/2014/07/translating-baghdadis-declaration-expelling-christians-mosul/.

11. 2 Corinthians 4:8–12.

12. Jonah 4:11.

Chapter 2

1. It's unclear from the translation exactly how much the surgery would cost. We think he said $15,000, but it could be more or less. It most certainly was in the thousands.

2. Catholic Online, "'Convert Right Now or We Will Kill Your Children in Front of You,' Baghdad Vicar Heard," Catholic Online, October 10, 2014, http://www.catholic.org/news/international/middle_east/story.php?id=57249. Some have disputed the claim that ISIS is beheading children because of a limited amount of photographic evidence. However, there have been repeated and

frequent reports. So I chose to leave this in the book, especially since I know Canon White so well.

3. Scott Wong, "Feinstein: ISIS Is Beheading Children," *The Hill*, September 21, 2014, http://thehill.com/policy/defense/218441-feinstein-isis-is-beheading-children. Several scholars have questioned the accuracy of Feinstein's statement. Some saying that it is ridiculous. I left it in the book because it is in the public record, and ISIS has committed innumerable and similar atrocities. So if this one isn't true, there are dozens of equally brutal stories that are.

4. Alice Spiri, "ISIS Reportedly Executed Children as Young as One in Syria," Vice News, June 6, https://news.vice.com/article/isis-reportedly-executed-children-as-young-as-one-in-syria.

5. "Syria: ISIS Tortured Kobani Child Hostages," Human Rights Watch, November 4, 2014, http://www.hrw.org/news/2014/11/04/syria-isis-tortured-kobani-child-hostages.

6. Omar Abdullah, "ISIS Teaches Children How to Behead in Training Camps," ABC News, September 6, 2014, http://abcnews.go.com/International/isis-teaches-children-behead-training-camps/story?id=25303940.

7. Cassandra Vinograd, "ISIS Trains Child Soldiers at Camps for 'Cubs of the Islamic State,'" NBC News, November 7, 2014, http://www.nbcnews.com/storyline/isis-terror/isis-trains-child-soldiers-camps-cubs-islamic-state-n241821.

8. Ibid.

9. Office of the High Commissioner for Human Rights and United Nations Assistance Mission for Iraq Human Rights Office, "Report on the Protection of Civilians in Armed Conflict in Iraq: 6 July–10 September 2014," http://www.ohchr.org/Documents/Countries/IQ/UNAMI_OHCHR_POC_Report_FINAL_6July_10September2014.pdf.

Chapter 3

1. Mary Chastain, "ISIS Soldiers Laugh, Joke About Buying Female Yazidi Slaves," *Breitbart*, November 3,

2014, http://www.breitbart.com/Big-Peace/2014/11/03/
ISIS-Soldiers-Laugh-Joke-About-Buying-Female-Yazidi-Slaves.

2. "Isil Carried Out Massacres and Mass Sexual Enslavement of
Yazidis, UN Confirms," *The Telegraph*, Richard Spencer, *Telegraph*,
October 14, 2014, http://www.telegraph.co.uk/news/worldnews/
islamic-state/11160906/Isil-carried-out-massacres-and-mass-sexual-
enslavement-of-Yazidis-UN-confirms.html.

3. Abdelhak Mamoun, "Exclusive: ISIS Document Sets
Prices of Christian and Yazidi Slaves," *Iraqi News*,
November 3, 2014, http://www.iraqinews.com/features/
exclusive-isis-document-sets-prices-christian-yazidi-slaves/.

4. Ahmed Rasheed, "Exclusive: Iraq Says Islamic State Killed
500 Yazidis, Buried Some Victims Alive," *Reuters*, August
10, 2014, http://www.reuters.com/article/2014/08/10/
us-iraq-security-yazidis-killings-idUSKBN0GA0FF20140810.

5. Steve Hopkins, "Full Horror of the Yazidis Who Didn't Escape
Mount Sinjar: UN Confirms 5,000 Men Were Executed and
7,000 Women Are Now Kept as Sex Slaves," *Daily Mail*, October
14, 2014, http://www.dailymail.co.uk/news/article-2792552/
full-horror-yazidis-didn-t-escape-mount-sinjar-confirms-5-000-men-
executed-7-000-women-kept-sex-slaves.html.

6. "The Revival of Slavery Before the Hour," *Dabiq*, 4, http://media.
clarionproject.org/files/islamic-state/islamic-state-isis-magazine-Issue-
4-the-failed-crusade.pdf, 17. This publication contains very graphic
and disturbing images.

7. Ibid.

8. Rose Troup Buchanan, "Life Under Isis: Captured Teenage Girl Tells
Story of Horrendous Abuse at Hands of Islamic State Militants,"
Independent, September 9, 2014, http://www.independent.co.uk/news/
world/middle-east/life-under-isis-captured-teenage-girl-tells-story-of-
horrendous-abuse-at-the-hands-of-islamic-state-militants-9721746.html.

9. Azam Ahmed, "In Retaking of Iraqi Dam, Evidence of
American Impact," *New York Times*, August 19, 2014,
http://www.nytimes.com/2014/08/20/world/middleeast/

in-retaking-of-iraqi-dam-evidence-of-american-impact.html?module=
Search&mabReward=relbias%3Aw%2C%7B%221%22%3A%.

10. Haleh Esfandiari, "ISIS's Cruelty Toward Women
Gets Scant Attention," *Wall Street Journal*, September
2, 2014, http://blogs.wsj.com/washwire/2014/09/02/
isiss-cruelty-toward-women-gets-scant-attention/.

11. Ibid.

12. United Nations, Independent International Commission of Inquiry
on the Syrian Arab Republic, "Rule of Terror: Living Under ISIS
in Syria," November 14, 2014, http://www.ohchr.org/Documents/
HRBodies/HRCouncil/CoISyria/HRC_CRP_ISIS_14Nov2014.pdf.

13. Alexander Smith, "ISIS Militants Hunt Down, Publicly Execute
Former Election Candidates," NBCNews.com, November 29, 2014,
http://www.nbcnews.com/storyline/isis-terror/isis-militants-hunt-
down-publicly-execute-former-election-candidates-n257616.

14. Office of the High Commissioner for Human Rights and
United Nations Assistance Mission for Iraq Human Rights
Office, "Report on the Protection of Civilians in Armed
Conflict: 6 July –10 September 2014," http://www.ohchr.org/
Documents/Countries/IQ/UNAMI_OHCHR_POC_Report_
FINAL_6July_10September2014.pdf.

15. "Isis 'Threatens to Execute Male Teachers Who Teach Female
Students,'" *International Business Times*, October 25, 2014, http://
www.ibtimes.co.uk/isis-threatens-execute-male-teachers-who-teach-
female-students-1471755.

16. Yifat Susskind, "Under Isis, Iraqi Women Again Face and Old
Nightmare: Violence and Repression," *Guardian*, July 3, 2014, http://
www.theguardian.com/global-development/poverty-matters/2014/
jul/03/isis-iraqi-women-rape-violence-repression.

17. Ibid.

Chapter 4

1. You will notice that once again I chose to use the word "ISIS" here
instead of "Muslim," because I do not believe for a single second that

the perverted ideology of ISIS is indicative of the Islamic faith shared by more than one billion people around the world.

2. Ignatius of Antioch, "The Epistle of Ignatius to the Romans," in *The Ante-Nicene Fathers: Translations of the Writings of the Fathers down to A.D. 325*, ed. Rev. Alexander Roberts and James Donaldson, vol. 1 (New York: Charles Scribner and Sons, 1903), 75.

3. These are almost exactly the same words she told me: http://gretawire.foxnewsinsider.com/2014/08/14/ iraqi-christian-nuns-plea-to-americans-care-for-your-christian-brothers-and-sisters-that-are-suffering-our-children-are-dying/.

4. "Dr. Seiple Accepts Invitation to Chair World Economic Forum's Council on the Role of Faith," Institute for Global Engagement, May 16, 2014, https://globalengage.org/news-media/press-release/ dr.-seiple-accepts-invitation-to-chair-world-economic-forums-council-on-the.

Chapter 5

1. John Lehmann, "Let's Be Honest: Man Haron Monis Was an IS Terrorist," *Daily Telegraph*, December 17, 2014, http://www. dailytelegraph.com.au/news/opinion/lets-be-honest-man-haron-monis-was-an-is-terrorist/story-fni0cwl5-1227158489614?nk=54d8b7 809901cca0b35c37da25bb1fac.

2. Chris Hughes and Richard Smith, "'ISIS Runaway' Yura Hussien May Have Been Lured to Syria by Jihadi Dating Site," *Mirror*, October 1, 2014, http://www.mirror.co.uk/news/uk-news/ isis-runaway-yusra-hussien-been-4361896.

3. Tribune Wire Reports, "Google: YouTube Overloaded With Terrorist Propoganda," January 28, 2015, http://www.chicagotribune.com/ news/nationworld/chi-youtube-terrorist-propaganda-20150128-story. html.

4. Shiv Malik, "Support for Isis Stronger in Arabic Social Media in Europe than in Syria," Guardian, November 28, 2014, http://www.theguardian.com/world/2014/nov/28/ support-isis-stronger-arabic-social-media-europe-us-than-syria.

5. Abraham Lincoln, "The Perpetuation of Our Political Institutions: Address Before the Young Men's Lyceum of Springfield, Illinois," in Joseph R. Fornieri, *The Language of Liberty: The Political Speeches and Writings of Abraham Lincoln* (Washington, DC: Regnery Publishing, 2009), 27.

6. "Pearl Harbor: Day of Infamy," Military.com, http://www.military.com/Resources/HistorySubmittedFileView?file=history_pearlharbor.htm.

7. CNN Library, "September 11th Fast Facts," September 8, 2014, CNN.com, http://www.cnn.com/2013/07/27/us/september-11-anniversary-fast-facts/.

8. Brian Michael Jenkiins, "The New Age of Terrorism," *McGraw-Hill Homeland Security Handbook* (New York: McGraw-Hill, 2006), 123; repr, RAND Corporation, http://www.prgs.edu/content/dam/rand/pubs/reprints/2006/RAND_RP1215.pdf, 8.

9. CBSNewYork/AP, "NYPD: Man Who Attacked Cops in Queens With Hatchet Was a 'Self-Radicalized' Muslim Convert," CBSNewYork, October 24, 2014, http://newyork.cbslocal.com/2014/10/24/nypd-officer-critical-but-stable-after-hatchet-attack-in-queens/.

10. Amikam Nachmani, *Europe and Its Muslim Minorities: Aspects of Conflict, Attempts at Accord* (Portland: Sussex Academic Press, 2010), 35.

11. "Table: Muslim Population by Country," Pew Research Center, January 27, 2011, http://www.pewforum.org/2011/01/27/table-muslim-population-by-country/.

12. Randall Palmer, David Ljunggren, Leah Schnurr, "Canada Parliament Gunman Had Planned to Travel to Syria: Police," *Reuters*, October 23, 2014, http://www.reuters.com/article/2014/10/23/us-canada-attacks-shooting-idUSKCN0IB1PY20141023.

13. Claire Adida, David Laitin, and Marie-Anne Valfort, "Terror in France: Implications for Muslim Integration," *Washington Post*, January 14, 2015, http://www.washingtonpost.com/blogs/monkey-cage/wp/2015/01/14/terror-in-france-implications-for-muslim-integration/.

14. Sara Wallace Goodman, "The Root Problem of Muslim Integration in Britain Is Alienation," *Washington Post*, October 6, 2014, http://www.washingtonpost.com/blogs/monkey-cage/wp/2014/10/06/the-root-problem-of-muslim-integration-in-britain-is-alienation/.

15. Charles C. Ryrie, *The Ryrie Study Bible* (Chicago, IL: Moody Press, 1976), 1376.

16. *Encyclopaedia Britannica Online*, s. v. "Caliphate," http://www.britannica.com/EBchecked/topic/89739/Caliphate.

17. "What's the Appeal of a Caliphate?" BBC *News Magazine*, October 25, 2014, http://www.bbc.com/news/magazine-29761018.

18. Ibid.

19. Ibid.

20. Jomana Karadsheh, Jim Sciutto, and Laura Smith-Spark, "How Foreign Fighters Are Swelling ISIS Ranks in Startling Numbers," CNN.com, September 14, 2014, http://www.cnn.com/2014/09/12/world/meast/isis-numbers/.

21. Holly Yan, "Why Is ISIS So Successful at Luring Westerners?" CNN.com, October 7, 2014, http://www.cnn.com/2014/10/07/world/isis-western-draw/.

22. *Wikipedia*, s. v. "1993 World Trade Center bombing," http://en.wikipedia.org/wiki/1993_World_Trade_Center_bombing.

23. Ibid.

24. Scott Bronstein and Drew Griffin, "Self-funded and Deep-rooted: How ISIS Makes Its Millions," CNN.com, October 7, 2014, http://www.cnn.com/2014/10/06/world/meast/isis-funding/.

25. Brett Logiurato, "ISIS Is Making an Absurd Amount of Money on Ransom Payments and Black-Market Oil Sales," *Business Insider*, October 23, 2014, http://www.businessinsider.com/isis-ransoms-20-million-treasury-says-2014-10.

Chapter 6

1. The Cradle Fund was founded in October 2014. Its first distribution occurred in December 2014. That first distribution provided direct assistance to more than seventy-two thousand individuals, and literally helped tens of thousands of them survive the harsh Iraqi winter.

2. Hobart E. Freeman, *An Introduction to the Old Testament Prophets* (Chicago IL: Moody Press, 1968), 273.
3. Johnnie Moore, *What Am I Supposed to Do with My Life?: God's Will Demystified* (Nashville, TN: Thomas Nelson, 2014), 73.

Chapter 7

1. *The Zondervan Pictorial Encyclopedia of the Bible*, Merrill C. Tenney, General Editor (Grand Rapids, MI: Zondervan Publishing, 1975), 1:372.
2. Will Durant, *Our Oriental Heritage* (New York, NY: Simon and Schuster, 1954), 264.
3. Kenneth Boa, *Talk Through the Bible* (Nashville, TN: Thomas Nelson Publishers, 1983), 268.
4. Ibid., 268.
5. Charles H. Dyer, "Ezekiel" *The Bible Knowledge Commentary* (Victor Books, 1985), 1225-6.
6. F.F. Bruce, *New Testament History* (Garden City, NY: Anchor Books, 1969), 368.
7. "Persecution and Religious Cleansing of Christians in Iraq and Syria," a Paper prepared by Nina Shea, Director of Hudson Institute Center for Religious Freedom, July 15, 2014.
8. www.ChristianityToday.com, "Mosul Islamist Takeover," June 10, 2014.
9. Joel S. Baden and Candida Moss, "Does Jonah's Tomb Signal the Death of Christianity in Iraq?" CNN.com, July 25, 2014, http://religion.blogs.cnn.com/2014/07/25/jonahs-tomb-and-the-collapse-of-christianity-in-iraq/.

Chapter 8

1. Much of this chapter is owed to a lecture given by Dr. Phillip Jenkins at Pepperdine University on April 9th, 2009. In part, he is quoted. In other parts, he is summarized. And in its entirety, you'll find his influence. Dr. Jenkins has given us the only significant scholarship in this space in recent times, and his impeccable work is of incalculable value to the salvation of these ancient Christian populations who

are largely unknown to the Western world. I am entirely indebted to Dr. Jenkins for my own understanding of this subject, and of this chapter. The lecture can be viewed here: https://www.youtube.com/watch?v=PVxq13lQESY.

2. At points, the preceding includes Dr. Jenkins' exact words from the aforementioned lecture, and at other points he is summarized. My notes from his lecture are imprecise, so I am not always clear on what he said verses my commentary on it.

3. Dr. Phillip Jenkins, *The Lost History of Christianity* (New York, NY: Harper One, 2008), 50–51.

4. Hobart E. Freeman, *op. cit.*, 228.

5. David Luckenbill, *Ancient Records of Assyria and Babylonia, Two Volumes* (Chicago, IL: University of Chicago Press, 1926–7), 1:148

6. Ibid., ix.

7. Ibid., x.

8. This is story is adapted from Dr. Jenkins' lecture. At points is summarized, and at other points I use his exact language. There are some variances from Dr. Jenkins' exact telling of the story.

9. www.history.com/topics/Charlemagne.

10. op. cit., 5–6.

11. Ibid., 71–72.

12. Chris Seiple, "Crisis in the Cradle of Christianity: A Strategy to Rescue, Restore, and Return," Institute for Global Engagement, October 23, 2014, https://globalengage.org/news-media/from-the-president/crisis-in-the-cradle-of-christianity-a-strategy-to-rescue-restore-return.

13. Remarks delivered by Cardinal Donald Wuerl at the Catholic University Mass of the Holy Spirit on August 28, 2014.

ABOUT THE AUTHOR

E xecutive, faith leader, author, speaker, and former senior vice president of one of the world's largest universities (of more than one hundred and twenty thousand students), Johnnie Moore has been called one of the most influential young leaders in the world today, and he is numbered among America's leading spokespersons for international religious freedom. At Liberty University, he led and spoke weekly to North America's largest regular gathering of Christian students.

Johnnie is chiefly a humanitarian whose adventures have taken him to more than two dozen nations. He's worked with genocide victims in Bosnia and Rwanda, established a sustainable agricultural project in economically downtrodden Zimbabwe, learned Buddhism from the Dalai Lama's personal archivist in the Himalayas, visited the world's largest refugee camps on the borders between Kenya and Somalia and Jordan and Syria, observed Hindu rituals on the banks of the Ganges River, and witnessed more than two thousand Asian Christians take a martyr's oath before receiving their college diploma. On five different occasions he has visited places that were later bombed by Islamic extremists. He is currently exclusively focused on the prolonged conflict in Iraq and Syria, and providing immediate assistance to the hundreds of thousands of displaced Christians, Yazidis, and other religious minorities through The Cradle Fund (www.cradlefund.org).

His diverse career has prompted leaders in education, politics, entertainment, and religion to consult with Moore on the challenge of translating their message and preparing their organizations for the rise of America's eighty million millennials. In a major profile of Moore's work, *The Washington Post* said, "Johnnie Moore speaks the language of young evangelicals."

He has worked with every major print and broadcast outlet in North America and written for various international media outlets, including CNN and Fox News. PR News recognized Johnnie as one of the top young public relations executives in America, and *Christianity Today* designated him as a "who's next" leader among the next generation of Christian leaders. His four books have received in excess of one hundred endorsements from some of the most influential faith leaders in the world.